THE IRISH QUESTION
AND BRITISH POLITICS
1868–1996

British History in Perspective
General Editor: Jeremy Black

PUBLISHED TITLES

THE IRISH QUESTION AND BRITISH POLITICS, 1868–1996

SECOND EDITION

D. G. BOYCE

Published in Great Britain by
MACMILLAN PRESS LTD
Houndmills, Basingstoke, Hampshire RG21 6XS
and London
Companies and representatives
throughout the world

A catalogue record for this book is available
from the British Library.

First edition 1988
Reprinted 1990, 1993, 1995
Second edition 1996

ISBN 0–333–66529–5 hardcover
ISBN 0–333–66530–9 paperback

First published in the United States of America 1996 by

ST. MARTIN'S PRESS, INC.,
Scholarly and Reference Division,
175 Fifth Avenue, New York, N.Y. 10010

ISBN 0–312–16109–9

Library of Congress Cataloging-in-Publication Data
Boyce, David George, 1942–
The Irish question and British politics, 1868–1996 / D. G. Boyce. –
– 2nd ed.
p.   cm. — (British history in perspective)
Includes bibliographical references and index.
ISBN 0–312–16109–9
1. Ireland—Politics and government—20th century.   2. Ireland–
–Politics and government—1837–1901.   3. Northern Ireland—Politics
and government—1969–1994.   4. Great Britain—Politics and
government—20th century.   5. Great Britain—Politics and
government—1837–1901.   6. Great Britain—Foreign relations–
Ireland.   7. Ireland—Foreign relations—Great Britain.   8. Irish
question.   I. Title.   II. Series.
DA959.B69   1996
941.508—dc20   96–11513
                                                                      CIP

10   9   8   7   6   5   4   3   2   1
05   04   03   02   01   00   99   98   97   96

Printed in Hong Kong

What then is the duty of an English Minister? To effect by his policy all those changes · which a revolution would effect by force.

(Benjamin Disraeli)

Much difference of opinion prevails as to . . . what the people of England could be brought to consent, and what the people of Ireland would be content to receive.

(Charles Greville)

Ireland under the Act of Union represented the government of one people through the public opinion of another.

(T. P. O'Connor)

CONTENTS

Contents

PREFACE

This is not yet another book about the 'Irish Question'. If it were it would (depending on the point of view) be much longer, and concerned with timeless verities like morality, justice and possibly original sin. Or shorter, since most of life in Ireland since life began there is not, contrary to popular opinion, concerned with 'Questions' – or even questions. This book is concerned with a theme that is at once wider and narrower than the Irish experience. It traces the role of Irish political affairs in British politics, and the response of British politicians to these as they impinged upon their world. It offers no model, colonial, quasi-colonial, neo, post or any other colonial. It avoids discussions of abstractions which owe more to the current state of Irish political conflict than to the realities of the Anglo-Irish relationship. Nevertheless, like all history, it is influenced by the time and conditions in which it is written. Historians are becoming aware of the need to redefine and reconsider what often passes for British (in reality English or even southern English) history and it is hoped that this book will make a small contribution to that large, and long overdue, exercise.

D. G. BOYCE

ACKNOWLEDGEMENTS

I am grateful to Mrs Pat Yates, Mrs Judith Gilbody and Mrs Phyllis Hancock for typing and retyping the manuscript, to Mr Chris Ince for designing and drawing the maps and to my family for their support. This book is for Patrick Buckland to thank him, however insufficiently, for his help and inspiration in Irish studies over some twenty years.

September 1987   D. G. BOYCE

IRELAND & GREAT BRITAIN

N

Glasgow
R. Clyde

R. Mersey
Liverpool

Bristol

North Channel

Londonderry
R. Foyle
ULSTER
R. Bann
R. Lagan
Belfast
Dundalk
R. Boyne

IRISH SEA

CONNAUGHT

R. Liffey
Dublin
LEINSTER

St George's Channel

MUNSTER
R. Lee
Cork

Scale (population)

100,000
50,000
10,000

Catholic
Non-Catholic

Counties
1 Antrim
2 Armagh
3 Cavan
4 Donegal
5 Down
6 Fermanagh
7 Londonderry
8 Monaghan
9 Tyrone
10 Londonderry
11 Belfast C.B.

N

Belfast

Newry

Londonderry

Boundary of six counties

0   50   100 km

RELIGIOUS AFFILIATION IN ULSTER, 1911

INTRODUCTION

THE OLDEST QUESTION: IRELAND IN BRITISH POLITICS AND HISTORY

I

The time when the Irish Question first entered British politics can be dated precisely. On 13 February 1844 the House of Commons began a nine-day debate on Ireland on a motion by Lord John Russell, who made a forceful speech on the theme that 'Ireland is occupied not governed'. The motion was defeated; but the importance of the debate lay in the recognition of Ireland as a special area, with a particular character, which required special treatment. These problems were summed up by Disraeli as 'a starving population, an absentee aristocracy, and an alien church, and, in addition, the weakest executive in the world'. The exactness of his definition may be open to question; but the point was, as the diarist Charles Greville noted, the 'very remarkable change in the tone and temper in which the Irish discussion was carried on'. The debate, he thought, revealed that the majority of MPs was 'impressed with the necessity of laying the foundation of a real and permanent union between the two countries'. But the difficulty, as Greville remarked, lay in the 'difference of opinion . . . as to . . . what the people of England could be brought to consent, and what the people of Ireland would be content to receive'.[1] The recognition that Ireland required what Disraeli called a 'revolution' effected through English policy;[2] and the difference between what England could consent, and Ireland be contented to receive, was the essence of the Irish Question in British politics.

Britain's approach to her newly defined Irish Question would be determined by the exigencies of her own politics; for the very definition of an 'Irish Question' placed Irish affairs in a category of their own, and politicians' inclination to 'do something for Ireland' depended very much on the state of public opinion in Britain, and at Westminster. It was in many ways easier to talk about Ireland than to act. Yet it was dangerous also to neglect Ireland completely; and it was even more risky to rely upon the simple use of 'coercion' to keep Ireland quiet. Nineteenth-century English political thought was pervaded by a strong sense of 'liberal values'. These values included certain ideas about how Britain could, or could not, behave in the conduct of her public life. There could be no banning of political parties; mass meetings could hardly be forbidden, without great risk to the forbidders; the law courts were there to administer the common law and protect the British citizen, wherever his origin; free speech, a free press and public criticism were regarded as axiomatic. Such hallowed traditions might be suspended in Ireland, it was true; but only in the teeth of much political and public criticism, for 'Prussianism' was never acceptable to broad areas of public opinion. Cynics might say that this amounted to no more than the concealment of the mailed British fist in a velvet glove; but the British belief in reasonable government, consensus and fair play, even if dismissed as typical of hypocritical Albion, could and did prove embarrassing to a British government bent on enforcing 'firmness' in Ireland. Moreover, Ireland sent representatives to the British parliament; and unlike, say, North African representatives to the French assembly, these politicians made their mark, in debate, divisions and style. Finally, the British representative system rested upon a doctrine of the sovereignty of parliament, the acceptance of the view that parliament was competent to legislate on any subject. When to this was added the development of political party organisation and discipline after 1870, and the corresponding increase in executive power, it was clear that Britain could legislate for Ireland in ways that she could not legislate for remote colonies. Thus the theory and practice of the British constitution offered politicians opportunities which they could take to deal with Ireland; and the

British response to Ireland would indeed be a peculiarly British one, which must be accepted with all its limitations as well as its possibilities.

This is not to say of course that politicians carried such a coherent or ordered set of ideas around in their heads. They were creatures of whim and fashion, avoiders as much as seekers of political issues. But sometimes issues could not be avoided; sometimes, indeed, politicians felt it imperative that they should be tackled; and politicians carried, if not in their heads, then at least in their motor muscles, certain practices and precepts upon which their political conduct was based. Thus, no other country would have handled the kind of political problems that Ireland seemed to present to British politicians in the nineteenth and twentieth centuries the way the British did; but this is not necessarily to be taken as a compliment. Neither is it a complaint.

The spread of English government over the whole of the British Isles from the Middle Ages to the end of the seventeenth century is the more distant background against which the role of Ireland in British politics must be set. This was anything but a systematic conquest; had it been, then it might indeed be possible to speak of British politics in a monolithic way, without the embarrassment of having to take into account the strange doings of the more western and northern parts of the archipelago. Indeed, it was not strictly speaking a conquest at all, since in 1707 the Union between England and Scotland was the result of hard bargaining (but certainly with England holding the best cards), while that of Great Britain and Ireland in 1800 was produced only after determined political efforts on behalf of the British government to induce the Irish parliament to dissolve itself, in the wake of a bloody rebellion and civil war. Ireland was given direct (and substantial) representation at Westminster, had her established Church united with that of England, shared in the United Kingdom's national debt, but was left with a viceroy, a chief secretary and a peculiar administrative structure. Once these arrangements were made the hope and expectation was that Ireland, like Scotland and Wales, would cease to trouble – or at least would cease to trouble England. This sometimes meant that England had to make it worth the while of certain groups or even peoples from the united (but not absorbed) territories to support the Union; ways and means had to be provided to satisfy the wants of the Welsh gentry or the lowland Scots Presbyterians, or – and here the question first arose concerning Ireland and England – certain sets of people in Ireland.

But with what sets of Irish people did the interests of the whole United Kingdom lie? Here was the conundrum; for in 1800 there can be no doubt that the Union was intended by the Younger Pitt to give the Roman Catholic majority of Ireland certain political rights, notably the right to sit in parliament in London; but at the same time assurances were made to the Protestant minority, and more particularly the landed gentry whose parliament was politicised out of existence between 1799 and 1800, that the Union would secure them in the rights and safety that their own political control of Ireland could no longer guarantee. In Ireland, Roman Catholic, Anglican and Dissenter eyed each other with a mutual suspicion, and with (in their own eyes at least) mutually valid claims on the support and loyalty of the British government. No one in early nineteenth-century Britain could doubt that the landed gentry were the natural leaders of any civilised society, but the landed people of Ireland belonged to a Church that indeed claimed to be 'native' – the descendant of the ancient Irish Church of St Patrick – but whose claims were refuted by the Catholic majority who, apart from historic doubts about the validity of the Anglican assumption of historical descent, had the more immediate grievance of paying tithes to a minority Church to which they did not belong. The vigorous radicalisms characteristic of many Presbyterians in the late eighteenth century might yet prove a danger to the Union. And there was the mass of nation, the Roman Catholics, who were in the 1820s to be organised in a formidable political movement for Catholic Emancipation. The difficulty was that the United Kingdom could not offer Roman Catholics their place, or offer it to them quickly enough, to prevent the launching of Daniel O'Connell's Catholic Emancipation crusade, a crusade in which political demands were inextricably mixed with millenial ideas about the downfall of heretic power in Ireland, and the replacement of those who were 'up' by those who were 'down'. But even the politics of Emancipation were a long-standing British Question, albeit now one with an important and disturbing Irish dimension; and O'Connell's bargain with the Whigs in the 1830s, by which Benthamite and Whig notions of good and sound administration would be applied to Ireland, was again but an extension of British politics to Ireland, not the acknowledgement of an Irish Question in British politics.

It was Sir Robert Peel's important administration of 1841–47 that marked the departure. Following the great debate on Ireland in February 1844, Peel reminded his colleagues of how matters stood in 1793 and 1800 when reforms had to be forced on the government, and declared that his policy must not be simply one of coercion, but must seek to 'detach' from disaffection 'a considerable portion of the respectable and influential Roman Catholic population'.[3] But Peel's great policy of reconciliation foundered on British distaste of too many concessions to Roman Catholic opinion in Ireland, on Catholic suspicion of his educational policies and finally on the Great Famine of 1845–47 which soon brought down not only his government, but his party as well, and consigned the Irish Question to political limbo for some twenty years.

II

And yet, between 1844 and 1867, the lines or markers for future identification of the Irish Question were discernable. When British politicians or administrators pondered on Ireland, they found themselves invariably talking about land, religion and education. And underlying these particular remedies lay the wider, not always articulated problem; how could the Roman Catholic majority – now calling itself the 'Irish' nation – be reconciled to the Union, without violence being done to the Protestant minority and to the Protestant sentiment of the majority of the population of Great Britain?

In 1844–45 Roman Catholic education was on the agenda; after the Famine it was a series of land bills that MPs found themselves discussing; in the 1850s the question of the privileged position of the Anglican Church, and its establishment, came to the fore again. But as always, it was the political circumstances of the time that shaped any British response to Ireland; and after 1848 Britain had had enough of Ireland, until the shock of Fenian bombings in Great Britain provoked consternation and the opportunity for Gladstone to take up the policy of his great predecessor, Peel, and set out to pacify Ireland. Gladstone was, after all, in origin a Peelite; and it can be said without exaggeration that the whole British idea of conciliation and the making of a true Union between Britain and Ireland was but an extension and development of Peelite policy. This reawakening of Peelism was given an earlier nudge by a brute fact that caught up on the British public and politicians in 1861. The census of that year marked the emergence of the Roman Catholics of Ireland as an irreversible majority. Out of a total population in Ireland of five and three-quarter millions, Roman Catholics numbered four and a half millions.[4] Of course it had been recorded for some time that Catholics outnumbered Protestants in Ireland, but the Famine had clearly reduced drastically the poorest and most fertile elements in the Catholic population and government legislation might bring British purchasers of land flocking into the country; and some like *The Times* assumed that 'a Celtic Irishman' would be 'as rare in Connemara as is the Red Indian on the shores of Manhattan'.[5] Protestant evangelical prosletysing might complete the process. At any rate there was some uncertainty about the future composition of the Irish part of the Kingdom. But now that this was clearly determined, then in an age which saw the advance of self-conscious groups defined denominationally it was unlikely that the claims of the Irish Catholics could for long be set aside.

This must arouse great interest and concern in the British public and its politicians. For politics in the nineteenth century, while concerned with questions of poverty, of the two nations, the rich and the poor, was also deeply and almost obsessively focused on religious questions, on their own terms, for their own sake, and also as a dimension of social justice and reform. The extraordinary popular outburst over the Papal attempt to reintroduce a diocesal system into Great Britain in 1851 was a symptom of the capacity of religion to arouse political fervour. Citizenship in the United Kingdom was informally, as well as constitutionally, defined by religion; Church and State were part of the one constitutional settlement of 1688. Thus the claim of the Roman Catholics to at least some of the spoils of their majority status was inevitably an integral part of the business of the British legislature: though whether its duty was to oppose them or to concede to them depended of course on individual as well as party political opinion. Then again the question of land reform raised other subquestions of rights in property, and in an age when political power and landed property were synonymous, any attempt to alter the system by which land was held in Ireland would inevitably provoke a debate of a most serious kind in Great Britain. Finally, even when it came to questions of nationality and self-government between 1886 and 1914, these questions were not like those in the Empire or in Europe. Once again it was a matter of debate concerning the loyalty that could be expected from a religious majority whose political style was couched in anti-English and anti-British terms, and which indeed was Catholic and therefore outside the normally accepted definition of British citizenship.

For the question of Irish nationality, which in 1886 became the major political issue of the age when Gladstone brought forward his proposals of self-government (Home Rule) for Ireland, was one that was inextricably bound up with the future of the British constitution, and more important, the British nation. Land, religion and education were one thing; Home Rule, in however restricted a form (and the restrictions were not all that considerable when it came to matters of domestic government) provoked the slumbering genius of British nationalism. For the Protestants of Ireland it was something quite different from Church reform or government bans on Orange parades. It was a great leap forward into an uncertain and dangerous future. But for many sections of British opinion, the same applied. Ireland was part of the British and English historical experience. The Glorious Revolution, still a popular and revered subject in nineteenth-century political memory, brought Macaulay to the walls of Derry, there to muse upon the implications of the great siege for the triumph of English liberty in 1688–89. Ireland's politics, like Ireland's history, could not but have serious consequences for the British future; for where would Britain stand in a world of great states, if she were to foresake the course of her history, that history that had made Britain a united nation, and seek instead 'the disintegration of the United Kingdom into separate cantons'?[6]

The idea of British nationhood, that fertile and inventive mixture of Celtic imagination and insight, combined with Saxon realism and practical skills, might have remained an affair of the intellectuals, of the students of race, the cranks even, who developed such notions as a 'science' of race and people in the late Victorian age. But it was given political urgency when once again a Liberal government, however reluctantly, took up the Home Rule issue in 1912, and took it up after the most bitter constitutional conflict in British history since the seventeenth century. From the time of its devastating rejection at the polls in 1906 the Conservative and Unionist Party was a party in a most nervous and defensive mood. The new Liberal government was regarded, not as the natural, if unwanted, winner in a general election, which the Unionists must live with during its term of office; it was denounced privately and publicly as a 'Home Rule-Pro-Boer-Little-Englander-Socialist party',[7] unfit to govern the United Kingdom and the Empire. It was bent on attacking property, British power and the British Empire; it had destroyed the veto of the House of Lords in the 1911 parliament act, which was tantamount to revolution; and now it was bent on completing the destruction of the constitution by granting self-government to a disloyal part of the Kingdom over the heads of its loyal elements, the Irish and especially the Ulster Protestants. The question was now to be put to the test: was the United Kingdom inhabited by a single nation, however much regional or even patriotic differences might distinguish its component parts; or, as the Liberals would have it, was it one whose national distinctions made it essential that they should be given some constitutional recognition? Both Unionists and Liberals believed their policies were essential to strengthen the United Kingdom, and to secure the Empire.

It must not be supposed, however, that the government of Ireland was perpetually invested with a sense of crisis; nor that British political perception of Ireland was stuck fast in the stereotype of Home Rule versus Unionism. In 1904 and 1907, first the Unionists, and then the Liberals, sought less radical constitutional adjustments by granting a more limited measure of devolution. But these tentative moves towards a kind of unofficial bipartisan policy were frustrated by the fact that Irish political parties were not, after all, 'aliens' in the body politic, but part of the great political realignment of 1886: Liberal politicians, the Nonconformist Churches and Irish nationalists on the one hand; and British Conservatives, Liberal Unionists, and Irish Unionists on the other. These alliances, informal though they were, and occasionally irksome, were durable because they were not founded on the question of Ireland alone, but on the newly-defined character of the Unionist alignment as the defenders of capitalism, property and order, and the consequent definition of the opposition alignment as the assailants of these British virtues. When Joseph Chamberlain pointed out the issue as one of 'patriots' against 'politicians',[8] he aptly summed up the desperate mood that gripped the Unionist alliance.

III

The last phase of the politics of the Union came after 1916, when the transformation of the British party system, and the whole political atmosphere, opened the way for an Irish settlement that placed the Irish Question beyond the realm of domestic political controversy, even if it did not and could not remove Ireland entirely from the political agenda. What it did achieve was the management and containment of Irish issues by the British political elite, which was now able to disavow any direct responsibility for what went on in Ireland. Strategic and economic considerations were now the decisive factors in British perception of Ireland, despite the occasional criticisms, mainly from the Left, of the state of affairs in Northern Ireland, established by a British act of parliament in 1920, but now consigned to the unhappy

Irish political past. Some Unionists, like L. S. Amery, might look back in regret rather than anger, convinced that some different policy – perhaps the abolition of the Irish viceroyalty when the Union was made in 1800 – might have saved the day.[9] But most British Unionists indeed, most British politicians, preferred to put Ireland behind them. This is not to say that Irish issues disappeared altogether from the view of British politicians. And it is instructive to recall that in March 1938 Neville Chamberlain was as much preoccupied with Anglo-Irish as with Anglo-Italian or even Anglo-German relations, as he sought to appease the nationalist and irredentist country on Britain's western flank. But even when Ireland was involved in the comings and goings of Imperial and Commonwealth conferences; even when Northern Ireland surfaced with its problems of chronic unemployment and occasional sectarian conflict in the interwar years; yet it was not what it had been between 1886 and 1922, an essential part of the education of a whole generation of British politicians. More significant was the loss of intimacy as a result of the Anglo-Irish settlement of 1921; for now relations between Great Britain, Northern Ireland and the Irish Free State (from 1937 'Eire') assumed an internationalised aspect. They were after all conducted between three governments: an 'Imperial' government in London, a devolutionary government in Belfast and a Commonwealth government in Dublin. Irish MPs in the House of Commons were reduced to a mere handful. There were no more 'Irish nights'.

This distancing process was encouraged by World War II, in which Eire remained neutral, to the irritation of some sections of British political opinion. The withdrawal of Eire from the British Commonwealth in 1949 was greeted with a mixture of regret and anger; but it was hardly likely to produce a significant British political reaction, and certainly no crisis in British politics nor even in Anglo-Irish relations, where the Labour government of Clement Attlee saved Irish citizens living in Great Britain from the serious consequences of Irish sovereign independence, but earned some obloquy for itself by further protecting the place of Northern Ireland in the United Kingdom. With Ireland now indisputably a sovereign state, and Northern Ireland enjoying cordial relations with Labour as much as Conservative administrations (and not many Liberals around to remind them of the past they had to live down), it was possible to think of British politics without Ireland, and of Irish politics without Britain.

IV

The early 1960s, however, were an era in which Britain developed a receptive mood to liberal and democratic causes. It was also a time when investigative journalism, especially television journalism, became fashionable. British public opinion was in an optimistic mood: and this attitude coincided with the emergence of an articulate, well-organised, mainly Roman Catholic political movement in Northern Ireland, the civil rights movement, which spoke the language of British liberal democratic politics and adopted the methods of civil rights protest in the United States of America. Perhaps a Northern Irish Question, in its apparently new modern form, was not all that surprising. At least it could be regarded as very different from the old Irish Questions that had wracked British politics 100 years ago. This was, it seemed, no rerun of the old Home Rule battles, nor was it a nationalist challenge to the sovereignty of the United Kingdom parliament, since Roman Catholics were demanding their rights as British citizens, nothing less, but nothing more. Administrative, political, social and economic reform of an integral, but much neglected, part of the Kingdom was now on the agenda. There was, on the face of it, nothing specially 'Irish' about that.

Once this civil rights movement, and Ulster Unionist reaction to it, threw Northern Irish politics into crisis, and then almost into chaos, the British realised that, as one newspaper editorial put it, they were again 'up to our necks' in the Irish Question.[10] But that question was to be kept firmly within the neutral zone defined by 'bipartisanship': there would be no taking sides in this new phase of the Irish Question.

But there would be a search for a solution, albeit one undertaken with reluctance, and even distaste; and between 1969 and 1986 British politicians produced a lengthy list of reforms, proposals, green papers, white papers and major political initiatives from the Sunningdale Agreement of 1973 to the Hillsborough Agreement of 1985. These recent attempts at an Irish settlement, however, joined that long list of political blueprints since 1868: the disestablishment of the Church of Ireland; land reform; the first, second and third Home Rule bills of 1886–1912; the Home Rule Act of 1920; the Anglo-Irish Treaty of 1921; the Anglo-Irish Agreement of 1938; the Ireland Act of 1949. Political achievement so far could not match political intention.

The reason for this might lie in the political methods used to reach a settlement; or in the idea of 'a settlement' itself. British politicians worked in a British context, and, as T. P. O'Connor remarked, the government of Ireland was the government of one people through the public opinion of another.[11] And whether it was Gladstone's disestablishment or Home Rule policies, his land acts, Lloyd George's Government of Ireland Act, or any of the catalogue of British responses to Ireland, they were framed to satisfy and appease British as much, if not more, as Irish opinion. They were drawn up with an eye to their acceptability in England – in what Lord Rosebery in an unguarded moment called the 'predominant member of the partnership of the three kingdoms' – their reception abroad, and their implications for the interests of Great Britain, or the United Kingdom's interests (as defined in London).

In Ireland the perspective was very different: 'home rule' was, in Liberal eyes, a rational and moderate means of reconciling Ireland to the Union, and restoring a political role to her landed gentry; but in Catholic Ireland it was described as 'independence', 'freedom', the entering of the (Catholic) nation into the promised land, the bringing down of the Protestants, 'Harry's Breed'.[12] In Protestant Ulster, Home Rule was tantamount to destruction. Similarly, when James Callaghan went to Derry in the summer of 1969 he was regarded in British political circles as a mediator between contending groups. But in Catholic Derry he was hailed as the harbinger of a new phase in Northern Irish politics, when the British government would give the Unionists their long-deserved rebuke.

But it was not only the difficulty of reconciling two, or more, sets of public opinion that interrupted the 'plot which keeps reaching a certain point'.[13] The problem may have lain in the concept of political activity inherent in the idea of an 'Irish settlement itself': especially when the declared intention of achieving this goal necessitated, but seldom received, the will and application of British politicians and public: there were usually more pressing matters to attend to at 'home'. Politics may be a boundless and bottomless sea, essentially an open-ended activity; but Gladstone for his part did not subscribe to the idea that the boat must simply be kept on an even keel. And subsequent generations of British politicians have in turn embarked upon the quest for a final solution of a baffling problem, whose very lack of solution seems at variance with the British political tradition. Gladstone believed that, in the case of Ireland at least, politics had a destination, and the Irish Question a solution. In 1868 he pushed the boat of the Irish Question on to the sea of politics. To trace the voyage of that boat, its tempests and calms, its apparent landfalls, its near catastrophes, is the purpose of this book.

V

A study of the Irish Question and British politics represents the point at which two historical, as well as political, traditions intersect. Yet very often historical treatment of Ireland fails to acknowledge this fact. British history makes more sense if Ireland is left out, for it can then be seen as the foundation and growth of an English kingdom which, gradually (if not always peacefully), incorporated Wales and Scotland into its political, social and economic system. After all, David Lloyd George, a Welshman, became prime minister of the United Kingdom; Queen Victoria confessed to being a secret Jacobite and, together with Sir Walter Scott, helped create a romantic Scotland that English people could respond to. But neither Parnell nor de Valera sought or found a place in British political life; and Queen Victoria resisted any suggestion to found a royal residence in Ireland.

If Ireland was considered historically at all, it was in terms of a troublesome and alien irruption into the British body politic. And whereas Irish historians are reluctant to see their country's history in terms of 'questions', and rightly so, British historians find it difficult to see their neighbour's history and relationship in terms of anything else. No one could ignore the impact of the Irish Question on the political fortunes of the Liberal and Conservative Parties; nor could they help reflecting on the effect it had on the political careers of British statesmen from Gladstone to Lloyd George. The violent and tragic outcome of the nineteenth-century Anglo-Irish problem in 1921 encouraged the idea that the ending of the Irish crisis – that great central experience of British politics and politicians – was a blessed relief. The only cause for wonderment lay in Gladstone's commitment to Ireland – which must therefore surely have been the action of a political saint, or a policy conceived for personal and political advantage, otherwise it simply made no sense. And the other puzzle was why the British Conservative Party, the party of moderation and pragmatism, fought so hard to defend the Union, when they should have been concentrating on social reform and the other obvious major problems of the present century. History, as always, was read backwards.

Chapter 1 attempts to establish the genesis of Gladstonian Irish policy and the Conservative response to it at a time when British and Irish politics were so close that it is impossible to separate them. Chapter 2 discusses the consequences of the British definition of, and response to, the Irish Question, and especially that most controversial of issues: the partition of Ireland. Here the release of new material, and a more realistic appraisal of Britain's motives throws new light on her attempt to find some kind of resolution of the divisions that were deep-seated in Ireland; divisions that partition acknowledged rather than created, but the resolution of which must also conform to British interests. British policy in the last phase of the Union, between 1919 and 1922, was essentially pragmatic; and the changing nature of British party politics holds the key to Britain's Irish policy in the postwar world.

In 1922 British rule ended over most of Ireland. Unionist

14

historians lamented the failure of British government, which between the Act of Union and the Anglo-Irish Treaty was seen as a great experiment that went wrong. Nationalists saw it as a burden placed upon the Irish people from which most of them escaped in 1921. But neither could ignore it. Historians of Britain/England enjoyed a different perspective. They could console themselves with the reflection that a relationship that should have ended in 1886 at last ended in 1921, for the good of England as much as Ireland. As D. C. Sommervell remarked candidly in his *The British Empire*, published in 1930:

> From the days of Grattan's Volunteers down to the days of Michael Collins, Ireland secured for herself a disproportionate amount of the attention of British politicians and the British public. It is impossible to estimate to what extent social reforms required by the population of the larger island were held up by the insistent claims to attention of 'Irish unrest'.

This, he admitted, may not have been the fault of Ireland; but he had no doubt that 'whatever mistakes may henceforth be made in Ireland can only be made by Irishmen'.[14] Chapter 3 studies this much neglected period in Anglo-Irish relations between the Anglo-Irish Treaty and the Ireland Act of 1949, using more recent research, when the two states of Ireland went their increasingly separate ways in both a British and Commonwealth context: a development that was to have profound consequences both for their future and for the place of Irish issues in British politics.

British historians after 1945 became preoccupied with two great issues: the decline of British power and the rise of the welfare state.[15] This excluded Ireland, which hardly seemed relevant to the far-flung Empire or the making of the managed economy. Yet the questions of British power – challenged by Irish nationalists, and successfully challenged in 1916–21 – and welfarism – which could be seen as foreshadowed in the British attempts to rule Ireland firmly but fairly after 1886 – need not have excluded a consideration of Britain's relationship with Ireland. The fact was that Britain seemed more legitimate, more homogeneous after Ireland; and Ireland, or most of it, for that matter, seemed more legitimate and homogeneous after Britain. Moreover, the Irish historiographical tradition was a highly political one, lacking the kind of consensus and agreement about norms, values and even areas of interest taken for granted in British history. Sir Lewis Namier might ruffle historians' feathers by his excited discovery of the springs of eighteenth-century political behaviour; but his discoveries were not a matter of political controversy that, say, any revision of the impact of the penal laws in Ireland would provoke.[16] And whereas Britain had a ruling class, Ireland had an 'Ascendancy'.

Small wonder, then, that British historians on the whole steered clear of the politics and relationships of their neighbouring island. Irish history was seen as (at best) a separate compartment by historians who were encouraged to write books and draw up syllabuses about Britain in Europe as a prelude to European unity. This feeling of the 'otherness' of Ireland was reinforced by the political events in Northern Ireland in the late 1960s, when the Ulster Crisis seemed to provide no familiarity, no clear points of reference, for historians of modern Britain. Chapter 4 seeks to establish a framework of reference for British policy at a time when Northern Ireland appeared to be a political museum. Chapter 5 describes and analyses the developments in British policy towards Northern Ireland between the Anglo-Irish Agreement of 1985 and the present. The demands of political contingency as well as purpose are assessed, and the international dimension considered, in a decade in which Northern Ireland moved from an intensification of political violence to a sudden, welcome, but uneasy peace.

If the Irish Question has proved hard for the British political elite and public to comprehend, it cannot be said that British historians have always fared much better. British historians, reared in a secular culture and a 'progressive' historical tradition, have found it hard to come to terms with the phenomenon of religion in politics (seventeenth-century historians fared rather better). They stand on the edge of a 'crease in time'[17] – a gap in the British historical experience, and writing, that is hard to fill.

This gap needs to be filled. In an age when history is regarded as a central part of the school and university curriculum, and when the focus of attention is on 'British' history, the time has come for a reassessment of what constitutes British history in the first place. The history of the history of the Irish Question in British politics is but a small part of that overall reassessment; but it deserves attention, for it is part of the debate about what properly constitutes British history, and, for that matter, Irish history. Britain in the last century was a multinational state, as she still is today. It is time that her historians began to acknowledge this, and write multinational history.

1

A QUESTION OF DEFINITION, 1868–1908: GLADSTONIAN REFORM, HOME RULE AND THE UNIONIST RESPONSE

I

In March 1868 an Irish MP put forward a motion on the state of Ireland; and Gladstone took advantage of the occasion to declare that the Irish Church 'as a State Church, must cease to exist'. His political timing and choice of subject were both acute. In December Gladstone had confessed that the cause of Irish disestablishment 'may again lead the Liberal Party to Martyrdom'; but after Gladstone moved that the House go into committee on his disestablishment resolutions, and a governmental amendment acknowledging the necessity for considerable modifications in the temporalities of the Irish Church was defeated, Gladstone's motion was carried by a majority of 56. His resolutions setting out the heads of his proposed legislation were carried by even larger majorities. Disraeli resigned, and a general election held in November 1868 gave Gladstone a majority of 116 and a political slogan that was to dominate the rest of his political career: 'My mission is to pacify Ireland'.[1]

This marked the definition of the Irish Question in its modern form: for it crystallised the Peelite policy of attempting to modify, while at the same time maintaining, the Union between Great Britain and Ireland. Catholic Emancipation was, after all, a British question, given momentum by O'Connell's powerful campaign; repeal of the Union had been denied absolutely. But to maintain the Union, while yet altering the terms on which it was made, began a process which threw up various proposals that were declared by their inventors to hold out the possibility of an Irish 'settlement': disestablishment, land reform, Home Rule, administrative devolution were all the product of this political process.

The problems of Ireland, especially the discontent of Irish Roman Catholics at their position under the Union and specifically their resentment of the superior position of the Church of Ireland, a state church subscribed to by a minority of Irish Protestants only, were undeniable. But there was little incentive to make them a political issue. Three developments ensured that they moved from situation to issue in 1868.

There was the essential point that Gladstone had for some time taken an interest in Ireland, and especially the role of the Church of Ireland in exciting Roman Catholic resentment. In the 1860s Gladstone had conceived the rudiments of an Irish policy, based on disestablishment of the Church and also reform of the land system. This evolved alongside a change in attitude towards religious compulsion: the Bishop of Ely in 1868 noticed a move in society towards the idea of disestablishment, since a larger proportion of the people was alienated from the established Church, and those people were gaining political power.[2] Gladstone's political convictions were sharpened in 1867 when he was brooding over how he could revenge himself on Disraeli, who had 'dished' him over franchise reform, and left the Liberal ship becalmed. An attack on the established Church in Ireland (but not yet on its land system which might, as an assault on property, arouse divisions in the Whig wing of the Liberal Party) would unite Whig and Dissenter alike.[3] Finally, the disposition of the general public to admit that an Irish policy of some sort was opportune gathered sudden momentum after bomb explosions and other outrages in British cities in 1867, the work of the Fenian Brotherhood, an Irish secret society whose aim was the destruction of British rule in Ireland by force of arms. The government, press and public were taken by surprise: London was gripped by 'Fenian Fever'; no more was heard of strikes or picketing; and in 1869 Gladstone admitted privately that Fenianism both in Ireland and Great Britain had 'a very important influence on the question of the time for moving upon great questions of policy for Ireland'.[4]

The Fenian panic of 1867 was not the cause of Gladstone's decision to reform the Irish Church system; but politics is as much about timing – 'the time for moving upon great questions' – as about intention. Gladstone believed that the British public and parliament were more disposed to take seriously an Irish policy after the Fenians than before. Gladstone's convictions, long held; his political opportunity to realise them; and the chances of realising them all came together in 1869. Moreover, the state of British party politics itself was one where religion was the touchstone of political feeling: drink, education, as well as Irish disestablishment, involved religious sentiment, as Nonconformist, Anglican and Roman Catholic strove to inject their particular views into political legislation, or the prevention and frustration of legislation. The Conservatives under Disraeli sought to fight on the ground of the general desirability of national establishments; and (somewhat against Disraeli's political inclination) they needs must fight for the Church of Ireland on those grounds. Protestant dissent in Great Britain formed what some regarded as an unholy alliance with Irish Roman Catholics, giving propagandist strength to the Liberals, especially in Wales and Scotland. Gladstone's decision to go for disestablishment was vindicated. His Irish Church Act not only passed through the Commons, it even met the grudging assent of the Lords, fearful of a clash with the lower house so soon after the passing of the second reform act, which enabled the Liberals to claim that their Church reform had an overwhelming public support.

From 1 January 1871 the Irish Church became a voluntary body: its law, its jurisdiction and its property suffered reform. The procedure was carried out with great consideration for the Church as a body and for its members as individuals; but its significance for the place of Ireland in British politics, and for the future of the Irish Union, was less favourable to the Protestant position in Ireland. The Union of the two kingdoms of Great Britain and Ireland had included also the Union of the two Churches of the kingdoms: the ending of one national establishment might be taken as casting some doubt on the permanence of the Union itself. Moreover, Gladstone had not, after all, 'pacified' Ireland; indeed, his decision to disestablish only gave hope and incentive to Irish Catholic politics which had laboured in the 1860s all in vain to achieve even a modest measure of university legislation. Now they had suddenly glimpsed the promised land, with Gladstone cast in the role of Joshua.[5] The rapid rise of a nationalist party in the 1870s, and the corresponding decline of Liberalism in Ireland, demonstrated that concessions did not 'pacify' Ireland, if by that phrase was meant settle once and for all Roman Catholic political demands. Richard Chenevix Trench, Archbishop of Dublin, warned that disestablishment would be followed by the land question, for the possession of the soil of Ireland by Protestants was a much more impressive 'badge of conquest' than the Church; eventually England must take its stand on the Union, and 'some new Cromwell' would emerge.[6] It is unnecessary to accept this apocalyptic view to agree that as British policy undermined the Protestant position, and as the substance of Protestant ascendancy diminished, the incentive for Roman Catholics, and for the British government, and the opportunity for both, to do away with the form of Protestant ascendancy increased.

It was clear that British attitudes to Irish policy were shaped, not only by the merits of any such policy, but by the demonstration that such policies carried a general relevance for Britain as a whole, or for sections of British society: disestablishment would have remained a mere idea had it been put to the British people on the merits of 'justice for Ireland'. Justice for Ireland quickened interest in Great Britain because it could be linked with justice for religious groups like Welsh Nonconformists, whose enemy was equally the Anglican pastor. Local elements in Great Britain rallied to the Liberal side; yet these were local and regional rallies, and it was still possible in other places for a Liberal landowner to remain a Liberal and not feel the sharp wind of local Nonconformist dissent. Liberals gained the best of both worlds from disestablishment: discomfort for their enemies at no cost to themselves. There was no break in the Liberal ranks, and the Conservatives' attempts to rally the Protestant cry in Great

Britain failed. But this happy result of Gladstone's Irish policy was not to recur in the dramatic years of 1886 and 1893.

Gladstone had rallied general support in Great Britain for his attack on the Irish Church establishment, using his supreme grasp of moral language to give his policy wide appeal. The question of land might prove more difficult; but here again Gladstone could rely on local British support, since Welsh Nonconformists' second enemy was the squire – not that they would have separated the squire from the Anglican parson in their catalogue of political villainy. What Protestant Conservatives regarded as the unholy alliance of 'Cardinal Cullen with Knox and Manning with Wesley' survived their counter-propaganda; and the fact that the striking of a blow against the landowner was also to strike a blow against the local social order in Wales (and Scotland) enabled Gladstone to embark with confidence upon his second Irish policy: land reform.

The Irish Church Act itself embodied some modest alterations in the terms on which tenants who lived on Church land held their property, for they were given the option of buying their holdings, leaving three-quarters of the purchase money on mortgage at four per cent. Now Gladstone proceeded to formulate a second major policy, but with all the necessary caution that a British prime minister and party leader must observe. The wind of opinion, he felt, was still behind him; but winds could change, and there were many in his cabinet who would bridle at an attack on property, and whose doubts must be respected. He could rely on John Bright, whose instincts were to use the state to buy out the Irish landlords; but Bright was an ally of doubtful value, and Gladstone contented himself with a measure that corresponded with his own desire to make the Irish landlords a still potent social force, offering an element of stability to Irish society. His Land Act of 1870 was given an easy passage in parliament, and the general willingness in Britain to accept this (however modest) interference in property rights was mourned by Lord Dufferin, who reflected that 'the great mass of the English people would sacrifice the Irish landlords tomorrow, if they thought that by so doing they could tempt the Irish populace into acquiescing in their rule'.[7]

22

The 1870 Land Act offered more security for tenure, establishing by law the so-called 'Ulster custom', a vague concept but one which generally included the right of a tenant to sell his interest in his holding, to obtain reasonable compensation for any improvements he had made in his holding, and a fair certainty of freedom from eviction, since if he were evicted the tenant would be entitled to reasonable compensation. Where the Ulster custom was not acknowledged, then a tenant was afforded compensation for improvements on giving up his holding, and if he were evicted his landlord must pay him compensation for 'disturbance'. Bright's radicalism was given a sop by the inclusion of some small provision to enable a tenant to purchase his holding. The cabinet was unhappy about a major intervention between landlord and tenant, however, and would go nowhere near the statutory recognition of tenant right over the whole of Ireland. As it was the land act failed, since its provisions only benefited a minority of Irish tenant farmers, and put the burden of legal proof on the tenant who must convince a court that his tenancy was indeed subject to custom, and also that the rights he was seeking to establish at law were indeed part of the custom under which he held. A court of law might well find in favour of a landlord, and in any case litigation was more likely to prove difficult for a tenant than for a landlord.[8]

All this is hardly surprising when it is acknowledged that Gladstone was anxious not to destroy the power of the landlords, but rather to give it a more certain base; and that his cabinet consisted, as did all nineteenth-century cabinets, of men drawn from the ranks of the aristocracy and gentry. Nevertheless, Gladstone had mapped out two lines of approach to the Irish Question, and lumped them under the broad headings of 'justice for Ireland', and 'the government of Ireland according to Irish ideas'. Indeed, he had in a sense defined 'Irish ideas' as somehow integral to the ideas of the Roman Catholic majority in Ireland, which was not far from recognising them as in some sense the 'people' of Ireland (and Gladstone in 1891 openly acknowledged that the Nonconformists of Wales were the 'people of Wales').[9] It was true that the land act was followed hard upon by a coercion act to maintain order in the Irish countryside. But this could not undermine the importance of a major British political leader demonstrating not only that a British party could take up Irish issues, but could win for them public support. Yet there were two principles in operation here which might prove irreconcilable: support for Gladstonian Liberalism in Ireland came mainly from Roman Catholic voters, and in the general election of 1868 the Liberals won 66 seats in Ireland, as distinct from 50 in 1859. Roman Catholics could hope for further reforms from Gladstone, especially in the field of education. But if another Irish party put itself before its electorate, based upon the government of Ireland by Irish ideas, and showed itself willing to take up land and educational reform, and all in the Roman Catholic interest ('Justice for Ireland') then Liberals would have a hard fight to maintain any strong political position in Ireland. Such a party emerged with the foundation of the Home Government Association by Isaac Butt in 1870.

The Irish Question, or at least the educational aspect of it, indirectly contributed to the general election of 1874, a small warning that before a prime minister sought to put forward policies he needed to accomplish what had been done in 1868, that is combine his party's solidarity with a reasonable hope of a favourable response from Ireland. Gladstone's education act fulfilled neither of these conditions. Moreover, the disappointment felt among Irish Roman Catholics at the measure provoked a wider interest in the new Home Rule Party, which placed land and educational reform before self-government. In the election of January 1874 the party won 60 seats instead of the 30 they had expected. They now constituted themselves a 'separate and distinct party in the house of commons', and set out to play the political game at Westminster in the way that best suited their aims. Moreover, their victories were all in Roman Catholic areas of the country, and indeed it was a feature of Irish politics from the 1870s that many seats were no longer contested in elections: Home Rulers sat for Catholic constituencies, and anti-Home Rulers sat for Protestant ones. Thus Irish politics did not fit into the 'constituency' model in quite the same way as they had done in the past. Home Rulers came to Westminster to bargain for a specific set of people – which they defined as the 'Irish' people – holding a specific area of 'national' territory (Ireland).

But, as always, British political conditions dictated the opportunities for Irish political advancement, and indeed for Irish political behaviour. When Disraeli and the Conservatives took office in 1874 they declared themselves willing to administer the law in Ireland 'fairly' but they had no concept of an Irish Question.[10] There was considerable irritation at the tactics increasingly employed by the Home Rule MPs in parliament, especially under the leadership of Charles Stewart Parnell, who with a few colleagues set out to use the procedure of the House of Commons to prevent or hold up its business, especially in committee. Isaac Butt, however, still held the loyalty of his followers, and still used reason and debate in the belief that this must prevail and in any case was the only feasible tactic to use in the British political system; like Bagehot, he subscribed to the idea that while the British body politic was hot, its atoms were 'cool'. Still, Ireland had helped bring Disraeli to power, and it was appropriate that Ireland should facilitate his loss of power. In 1879 Ireland stumbled into an agrarian crisis that produced a dangerous and complex combination of agitation, violence and a united and powerful political leadership under Parnell and Michael Davitt, ready to exploit discontent and turn it to their advantage. Disraeli leapt into the dark in 1880 with a dissolution and a campaign of resisting Irish agitation and, above all, preventing Home Rule. Gladstone reaped the reward with a resounding victory at the polls. Something would have to be done about Ireland, but, wrote Earl Spencer complacently in March 1880, Home Rule would 'not be a difficult question for our party for we practically do not differ from the Tories on it. We wish the maintainance of the Imperial Parliament'.[11]

Gladstone began with land, which was by now almost an 'agreed reform' between British political parties. The general reaction to the 1870 act even among landlords was that 'it might be worse';[12] and when Gladstone took office in 1880 a royal commission appointed under his predecessor was already investigating the working of the 1870 act. Gladstone's instinct was to postpone any new legislation until this commission should report, and he exhibited some degree of complacency about the state of Ireland in his election address of March 1880.[13] But it is a travesty of Gladstone's politics to suggest that he was always inclined to wait upon events, or to ignore his capacity to learn from Irish MPs who pressed him strongly to bring some emergency measure to protect tenants greatly in arrears with their rent from eviction. Nevertheless any Irish legislation must inevitably meet the necessities of the British parliamentary process, and the House of Lords' rejection of the bill opened the way to an intensification of the Land League's campaign of agrarian disturbance. Yet the very intractability of Irish affairs only put Gladstone on his mettle, for it encouraged his conviction that, as he himself put it, the goodness of his intentions must prevail: 'it is impossible that acts of justice and goodwill should not bear fruit. If we lose faith in that principle, we lose faith in human nature'.[14] Gladstone's remark was made in the context of his introduction of an Irish coercion bill in 1871: and it is easy to dismiss it as hypocrisy. But Gladstone, although he acknowledged that it was necessary to meet disorder with coercion, and suspended habeas corpus in a bill passed in February 1881, was persuaded by his chief secretary for Ireland, W. E. Forster, to offer also a new land bill. This bill went much further than his 1870 measure, conceding the 'three F's': fair rent, to be assessed by arbitration; fixity of tenure while rent was paid; and freedom for the tenant to sell his occupancy at the best market price.

Gladstone's land act was open to several interpretations. In the context of British public opinion, it was, as Gladstone himself later admitted, made possible by the state of agrarian disorder in Ireland, which prepared the British public for measures of state intervention that would have otherwise been considered too adventurous, and which he himself had initially regarded as highly undesirable. In Ireland it seemed to indicate that disorder brought concession which order could not; indeed, this impression could be gleaned from British (which means Gladstonian) policy in Ireland since 1868. But constitutional politicians and the Roman Catholic Church were as anxious to get concessions to prevent or undermine the forces of disorder as any British politician. And this form of tacit understanding, collusion, or indeed cohabitation, explains the tortuous moves made by Gladstone between 1881 and 1884: for Parnell himself was anxious to maintain influence over the Land League and prevent it exceeding the kind of controlled disorder and boycotting that brought it to political prominence. Hence the Gladstonian coercion, violently denounced by Parnell, and negotiation, which Parnell had to enter into carefully lest it cost him support in Ireland. In April 1882 Parnell and Gladstone reached agreement, by which Parnell, who had been arrested in October 1881 under the Crimes Act, was released from gaol, coercion ended, the land act amended and tenants in arrears protected. Parnell suffered criticism from more determined agrarian radicals, and his agreement with Gladstone might have proved difficult to defend in Ireland. But matters took a dramatic turn following the murder in Phoenix Park of the newly appointed Lord Lieutenant, Lord Frederick Cavendish, and his assistant secretary, T. H. Burke, by the 'Invincibles', a band of assassins with which Parnell had no connection. Parnell's reaction was one of sincere and deep revulsion; but the subsequent collapse of his agreement with Gladstone enabled him to rise above the dangers inherent in 'collusion' with Britain, and in October 1882 he firmly established his power in nationalist Ireland by the foundation of a new body, the National League, which replaced the Land League, gave him a well-organised and widespread popular base, and offered him the chance to combine land and politics in a disciplined parliamentary party.

Violence, agitation, murder: all these inevitably seized the headlines in the British press, and have played a significant part in the British response to the Irish Question ever since. But in 1884–85 a change was made in the British constitution which was to have a notable impact on the character and role of the Irish Question in British politics until 1918. The government had promised in 1880 to tackle the franchise question, and particularly the necessity, perceived by both main parties, of extending the current household suffrage in the boroughs to the county constituencies. This was perhaps no more than a tidying up operation; but the question of any redistribution of seats was a more controversial one. It was eventually agreed that a franchise act would be passed first, with redistribution to follow. There were those in the cabinet who had reservations about the wisdom of extending this new measure of popular government to Ireland; but the caution with which earlier franchise reforms were applied to Ireland exercised no influence in the drafting of the new measures, and the Irish electorate increased in size from 4.4 per cent to 16 per cent of the population, with a reduction in borough representation. Parnell reaped the reward in the general election of 1885 when the Home Rulers won 85 seats, 17 of them in Ulster.

Parnell's parliamentary position was now at its strongest, cemented by the 'pledge' of 1884 which committed candidates, if elected, to vote with the party on all occasions when the majority decided that the party should act in unison. The Liberals, as the party in power, had to decide whether or not to renew the coercion legislation of 1882, which was due to lapse at the end of the parliamentary session in 1885, and they were reluctant to go to the country on a purely repressive policy. Parnell was looking for pickings from whatever British party seemed more likely to suit his purpose. There seemed a possibility that the Conservatives would be influenced by Lord Carnarvon, the new viceroy, who was known to hold views favourable to Home Rule;[15] and the Parnellites united with the Conservatives to defeat the government in June 1885. When the government went to the country in November 1885[16] Parnell urged the Irish voters in Great Britain to support the Tory side.[17] Within six months the Liberals were back with Parnellite support, and a bill for self-government in Ireland was laid before the House of Commons by Gladstone.

II

This remarkable reversal in the attitude of British political parties towards Home Rule, and especially Gladstone's conversion to the policy of Irish self-government, has occasioned much debate. The more sceptical have attributed it to Gladstone's bid to reassert his leadership over the Liberal Party, now threatened by new, younger radical leaders like Joseph Chamberlain. Gladstone's speeches are cited as examples of his earlier opposition to any such policy in an effort to deny any ideological dimension, or indeed any political consistency at all.[18] But those who cite Gladstone against himself, when he declared in 1871 that he intended the United Kingdom to 'remain a United Kingdom' (to the accompaniment of loud cheers) ignore the great distance that Gladstone had travelled, politically, by 1885. In 1871 Gladstone 'looked in vain for the setting forth of any practical scheme of policy' which the Imperial parliament could not deal with as well or better than any Home Rule legislature; by 1885 he had come to the conclusion that there were indeed 'practical schemes' that could only be worked out by Irishmen themselves.

Certainly Gladstone's oft-repeated desire to retire from politics, now postponed because of his conviction that he, and he alone, could settle Ireland, suggests a strong personal motive; and it is easy to portray him as an old man in a hurry to keep his job as leader of his party. But that personal motive, for Gladstone, transcended mere political ambition. It was deeply associated with ambition; but he found it not only agreeable, but imperative, to equate his own political future with the principle of great and good acts of government: only he could see what had to be done, and only he could do it. Therefore he must stay at his post. Moreover, Gladstone was capable of thinking out some general principles of policy which might then be applied if the moment was propitious. When Gladstone visited Ireland in 1877, receiving the freedom of the City of Dublin, he suddenly unmuzzled himself, and indicated two broad areas of policy concerning Ireland. One was that which he called 'local government, not only in the shape of municipal institutions, but in all those other shapes in which it is known to our history, is a thing . . . not to be viewed with misgiving'. Parliament was manifestly failing in the discharge of its duties; government was over-centralised. The Three Kingdoms (Ireland, Scotland and England) 'should be one nation to the face of the world', but the people should be trained in their public duties locally so that they could all the more effectively carry them out nationally. This was an extension of political liberty.

The second broad political area was land. Here Gladstone mused on the differences between England and Ireland. In England it was essential that the land should be owned by one set of men and tilled by another; and anyway the mass of the population did not desire to purchase the land. But Ireland was very different. The tenants needed security and confidence, and Gladstone declared that 'for my own part, attaching small importance to the acquisition of small proprieties in England, I attach great importance to it in Ireland'. It was of the greatest consequence: 'the creation of a class of small proprietary in Ireland will give new views and new ideas to the proprietors'. There was in Ireland a sharp division between the interests of the cultivators and those of the proprietors. 'The best cure for that is, that in a good and appreciable number of instances the same man shall be cultivator and proprietor too'. He then would learn to look at the whole case, and realise that there was no necessary conflict between these two classes, but that they ought 'mutually to assist and support one another'.

Having made these sallies, Gladstone then rather disingenuously ended by saying that he had 'advisedly refrained from entering on the politics of the future', but that the Liberal party, however much it had lost ground in the last two general elections in Ireland to the Home Rulers, would have its policies governed by the desire to obtain 'justice' for Ireland.[19] The fermentation of these ideas, necessarily vague and ill thought out, was a slow process; but by 1885 they were ripening. In August 1885, Gladstone read a memorandum to Lord Hartington in which he stated his belief that in Ireland there was:

> An epoch: possibly a crisis. Grievance in the main gone, but administrative development remains. Considerable changes may be desired; & may be desirable if effected with due regard to the unity of the Empire. I cannot treat the people of Ireland as foes or aliens, or advise that less shd be done for them than wd in like circumstances be done for the inhabitants of any other portion of the U.K. Those are my opinions.[20]

Now Gladstone believed that British public opinion was ready to take up this great political cause, if it was properly educated into acknowledging its importance. He was convinced that the British people were sick of 'coercion' in Ireland. There was therefore simply no other direction in which British policy could proceed. Moreover it must be remembered that when Gladstone first tackled, indeed defined, the Irish Question as one of religion and land, there were many Liberals sitting for Irish constituencies. By 1885 it was clearly the case that the Parnellites were the force to be reckoned with in Ireland.

But Gladstone still moved cautiously. He would reconcile the broader view, that Ireland must have 'justice', with the political conditions prevailing in 1885–86. Gladstone lost his majority in the House of Commons on 24 June 1885 after a defeat on the budget on 8 June, but he carried on as caretaker prime minister, a general election having been postponed so that the necessary changes to the electoral register caused by the recent franchise reforms could be made. He told Hartington on 3 September that Ireland 'has perplexed me much', but he warned than any premature disclosures would be dangerous, and pointed out that 'it is not what Parnell says now, but what Ireland will say or do at the election, that forms the call upon us for definite declarations'.[21] Nevertheless, Gladstone took the trouble to ascertain Parnell's views on an Irish constitution, and by the middle of November Gladstone had jotted down headings of a Home Rule measure. These laid down, in effect, the formula for Home Rule plans, measures and policies from 1886 until 1921: that an Irish chamber should be established to deal with 'Irish, as distinct from imperial questions'; that this required new fiscal arrangements between the Irish parliament and the imperial parliament; that Irish representation in the imperial parliament must be reconsidered.[22]

Gladstone still hoped, as late as December 1885, for a Tory-Irish alliance, even sketching out the strategy which Lord Salisbury should pursue, and the Liberal alternative should Salisbury then fall from power – and all this despite his son's disclosure in the press that Gladstone was now convinced of the need for Irish Home Rule.[23] But when the Conservatives declined to fill the role Gladstone designed for them, Salisbury's government was defeated in the Commons on 27 January 1886. Gladstone formed an administration which (he hoped) would enable Ireland to settle down peacefully and in an atmosphere of social stability under the sovereignty of the United Kingdom parliament, and with her landlords freed from the shackles of a historically unjust land system, participating fully in Irish politics as they had done in the late eighteenth century.

Gladstone had always been concerned about what he called the 'social order' in Ireland, as his speech in Dublin in 1877 testified. He had accepted that the special conditions prevailing in Ireland rendered the English system of landholding irrelevant there. Now he sought to settle the land question through the more radical policy of creating a peasant proprietary. This entailed using British money 'to the uttermost . . . on behalf of Ireland'[24] in order to buy out the landlords. Gladstone therefore linked the constitutional settlement to the land question; thus the state, and not the landlord, would be the recipient of rent. This, as he fully acknowledged, was a 'bribe' to the landlord, and an integral part of the whole Irish settlement;[25] a bribe made more attractive by the fact that, as Gladstone put it, 'it is doubtful whether the Irish Chamber [i.e. Home Rule parliament] could be trusted to treat him fairly'.[26]

Gladstone was always concerned about the difficulties of maintaining Liberal Party unity in the event of his adopting a policy of Home Rule, hence his unwillingness in the general election of November 1885 to make a specific declaration for Irish self-government when challenged by Parnell. Lord Hartington, unhappy about the new radical spirit abroad in Liberalism as well as Gladstone's Irish policy, and Joseph Chamberlain, an enthusiastic Radical but a convinced believer that Parnell's speeches and declarations could not be twisted in any other but a separatist way, fulfilled Gladstone's forebodings. Chamberlain had earlier advocated some measure of administrative devolution for Ireland. But there was always in his mind, and in the minds of others, a vital – and indeed real – distinction between allowing an Irish 'central board' to manage matters devolved to it by Westminster and a full-scale popularly elected Irish national parliament with an executive responsible to it, equipped with powers to make laws for Ireland on virtually all domestic matters, and with Irish MPs removed from the House of Commons.[27]

Parnell for his part had not expected anything as far-reaching as Gladstone's Home Rule bill. The best he had anticipated was some measure of local government reform.[28] But Parnell was now placed in a new position: the independence of his Irish party was at an end. Once Parnell committed himself to the Liberal alliance, once he accepted the conversion of Gladstone to Home Rule in 1886, he effectively ended such independent existence as the Irish Parliamentary Party ever enjoyed. The crisis left Gladstone with a weaker Liberal Party, and a weaker political base in England; but it recreated, though less powerfully, the old alliance of 1868-69: British Nonconformity, Irish nationalism and Gladstonian Liberalism. The Welsh Nonconformists supported Home Rule; the Irish Nationalists therefore sympathised with the disestablishment of the Church of Wales; and Gladstonian Liberalism took on a distinctly 'Celtic' flavour, with Gladstone hinting at Welsh Home Rule (but no more than hinting). It was not as strong an alliance as it had been fifteen years before, for the weakening hold of Gladstonian Liberalism on the largest part of the Kingdom, England, could not be compensated for in electoral terms: between 1886 and 1906 the Liberals held office only briefly, in 1892-95. But it was nonetheless a pan-British alliance that held together, despite its inherent weaknesses and political strains. The Irish Question had played a major part in British political alignments in 1886 – it would do so for the last time with its departure from the centre of the British political stage in 1922.

Gladstone believed that Ireland possessed what he called the elements of nationality: 'collective or corporate individuality, tested by reason, and sufficiently confirmed by history'. He further believed that the 'map of Europe shows us that in cases like those of Hungary or Norway, a vigorous sense of nationality is compatible with effective organic union tempered by autonomy'.[29] The alternative, Gladstone feared, was social chaos in Ireland and the undermining of the stability of the British political system. This was a sound conservative argument for the recognition of local autonomy, in which Ireland would follow the example of Scotland and settle down under British rule. But it was difficult for the Conservative Party to accept it, or to accept it on Irish terms. For here again the crisis of 1886 – its suddenness, the unexpected rise of the Irish Parliamentary Party,

33

its heightened role in the hung parliament of 1866 – all called for politicians to define what they had left vague, and to sum up what they had previously only half-investigated. There were those in the Tory Party like Lord Randolph Churchill who had been regarded by some as the likely creators of a Conservative Home Rule policy.[30] Some argued that the Conservative fight to uphold denominational education would find natural allies among the Irish Roman Catholics.[31] But the policy of Home Rule was of a different order from these matters. To Conservatives it appeared to be the destruction of the United Kingdom, not only because of the extremism of the measure (especially the proposed removal of Irish representation from Westminster) but because the Irish were not a loyal people – or at least their political leaders were not. Now the previous five years or more of agrarian agitation, moonlighting and terrorism were recalled to show that the Irish nationalists were the sworn and deadly enemies of the British and their Empire. Moreover the role of Ireland in British politics was different from before, because British politics were different: if the United Kingdom did not have democratic politics, or anything like that in a formal electoral sense, it did have popular politics. How would Home Rule fit into this political world? Lord Randolph Churchill gave an answer when he resolved to come out against Home Rule, and to make what he himself called an extremist speech on the subject.[32] But Salisbury himself knew that the era of popular politics had come to stay, and that Ireland could not be kept within the charmed circles of high politics, of the world of the political elite. Parnell was a popular political leader of a mass movement; his opponents must be likewise; and in opposition to the Nonconformist-Liberal-Nationalist alliance the Conservatives offered a predominantly English, British Nationalist and Protestant patriotic alliance, with a strong foothold in the province of Ulster.

It would be absurd to say that the Irish Question was an invention of British politicians; but it is true to say that their perception and definition of it changed the Irish situation, with all its complexities, into a simplified political form, and that the events of 1886 poured it into a mould which could not, apparently, be broken – a mould of 'home rule versus Unionism'.

Moreover, Gladstone's Home Rule policy produced an offshoot that was also the product of the British political perception of Ireland: the Ulster Question.

The first Home Rule bill simplified Irish politics: it forged the Nationalist-Liberal alliance that was to survive, despite splits in the Home Rule movement, until 1916; it swept away Ulster Liberalism; it created an alliance between Irish Unionists and British Conservatives, and especially it made Ulster the stronghold of uncompromising Unionist opinion. The less public part of this political arrangement – the influence of the southern Irish Unionists within the ranks of the Conservative Party and its Liberal Unionist allies – was as important as the more public championing of Ulster Unionism. It ensured that Irish Unionism was no mere hanger-on to the flank of a supportive but uncomprehending Conservative ally (an ally which had ignored their objections to the Marquis of Salisbury's acceptance of the Franchise and Redistribution Acts of 1884–85, which opened the way to Parnell's success in the general election of 1885), no mere opportunistic English connection with what Randolph Churchill dubbed the 'foul Ulster Tories', but an integral part of the whole Irish–British-Unionist front. Nevertheless, when the Conservatives wished to put the case against Home Rule before the British public, it was the Ulster Unionist case that they could more readily put: the spectacle of a definable, regional, Protestant people, industrious and loyal, placed under the heel of Her Majesty's enemies was a persuasive one.[33] The Liberals, through omission, also contributed to this sharpening and narrowing of the issue in British politics. Gladstone considered the case of those groups which might 'at first glance, be mistaken for signs of an historic nationality' such as the Basques. But he placed such groups on the same footing as the highlanders of Scotland 'before the assimilating measures of the reign of George III'. The highlanders had a separate language, traditions, usages and social habits; with these distinctions they 'joined a marked military superiority over their neighbours; yet the candid observer will feel that they did not possess the constituent conditions of a true historical nationality; and they have learned, recently, but fully, familiarly, and freely, to feel that they belong to the integral nationality of Scotland'.[34]

On these grounds, then, Ulster Protestants did not qualify for the approbation of history. And the general election of 1886 revealed the new alignment of United Kingdom politics, with the Irish nationalist, Welsh, Scottish Gladstonian axis confronting the predominantly English supported British Conservative, Liberal Unionist and Irish Unionist alliance. It would be a crude oversimplification to see this as the 'Celtic' lands ranged against the 'Saxon'; but often politics are about crude simplifications, and it was this wider racial aspect of the issue that made it more intractable. Whatever the nonsense talked (and still talked) about 'ethnicity' in Britain (two islands peopled by immigrants) nonetheless the notion of racial differences was one attractive to much Victorian thinking about politics; and the defence of the British nation against its Irish nationalist and (by proxy, by guilt association) its Liberal allies was one likely to raise the political temperature, especially in a world of increasing state consolidation, in Germany and in Italy, where a Balkanised Britain must sink, Darwin-like, to decay and decline.

III

Gladstone's appearance at the dispatch box in June 1886, at the age of 76 must excite as much interest today as it did when, in prophetic style, he urged his opponents to think 'not for the moment, but for the years that are to come'. His passionate oratory still obscures the flaws, constitutional and financial, in his Home Rule bill. But he was frustrated by the fact that, even if Ireland, or most of it, was ready for Home Rule in 1886, England was not. Gladstone hoped that his bill would be one of those political departures, which, taken at the flood, would combine political and public opinion in an irresistible movement towards his political goal. But it turned out to be a boat bobbing about on an uncertain political sea. The next twenty years were to see almost unbroken Conservative (or as it was now called, Unionist) rule, with a brief Liberal interlude.

Yet the Unionists were by no means a confident and assured party when it came to defining their Irish Question.
The Liberals could always claim that they stood for peace,
settlement and the winding up of an historic conflict, and but for
the scandal surrounding Parnell's citation in the O'Shea divorce
case in 1891 Gladstone's prospects for getting Home Rule
through the two houses of parliament were at least hopeful: had
Parnell's authority and reputation remained unsullied, then it
would have been more difficult for the House of Lords to reject
the second Home Rule bill without running the risk of a serious
confrontation with the Commons. The Unionists could offer
firmness (or coercion, to give it its more accurate description);
and what one historian has called the 'hardening during the last
third of the nineteenth century in Britain's moral culture'[35]
enabled the Unionists to use state coercion when appropriate,
and indeed to connive at, or encourage, the attempt made in
1887 to blacken Parnell's name by associating it with the
Phoenix Park murders. But no British political party, even in the
altering political climate, could simply stand upon coercion. And
in any case it was difficult in politics to stray too far from the
clearings already made, or in the making, of one's predecessors.
No sooner had the Unionists taken office in 1886 than they were,
by the beginning of 1887, revising the 1881 Land Act in the
tenants' interest, under the prompting of their new Liberal
Unionist colleague, Chamberlain, and much to Lord Salisbury's
disgust.

Gladstone had hoped in December 1885 that some kind of
forum for the discussion of Anglo-Irish relations might be de-
vised, or that in some way the two major British political parties
could reach a bipartisan agreement on Irish policy. He reflected
on the great political crises of the past, those of 1829, 1846, 1867,
when a Tory administration had enacted great and controversial
measures with Liberal or Whig support. The subsequent fate of
the cooperative Tories was one hardly likely to attract them to
this piece of noblesse oblige. But once this proved impossible,
once the Irish Question was defined as a party political question,
then it took on a momentum and a life inseparable from the
political battlefield. Unlike land legislation, Irish self-government

did not become an agreed reform; though a lesser measure of devolution was to look as if it might achieve that status after 1903. Even if it did, a perceptive observer might have considered the significance of the 'noises off' coming from the Unionist north of Ireland: the talk of arming and preparing to resist Home Rule to the last man.

Gladstone did not let his defeat over his first Home Rule bill cast him down; on the contrary, he declared in August 1886 that he was 'in Parliament to contribute if I can to the settlement of the Irish question'.[36] His wishes were to be fulfilled, in that the Irish question would not go away with the failure of Home Rule in 1886. Ireland claimed the attention of British politics for the rest of Gladstone's political career. Gladstone hoped to make Home Rule an acceptable, instead of an exceptional, strand of British political discussion; its opponents characterised it as a revolutionary break with the political history of the United Kingdom. By the late 1880s, Gladstone seemed on the point of achieving his goal: the Liberals would win the next general election, the tide of Home Rule was rising, and Parnell was vindicating Gladstone's prediction of an Ireland at peace with England through his policy of studied moderation, and, in particular, by distancing himself from the limited but trouble-some 'Plan of Campaign' – an attempt by some Home Rulers to revive agrarian agitation.

Gladstone therefore bent himself to his labours with a will. He met Parnell at Hawarden on 18–19 December 1889. He drafted a memorandum setting out changes that would be needed to his Home Rule bill. Detailed decisions about a future bill were set aside, perhaps because Gladstone did not want to give ammuni-tion to the Unionists. But all this was cast into jeopardy by the Captain O'Shea's divorce case which was initiated only five days after Gladstone and Parnell met at Hawarden. This case was decided on 17 November 1890, when Captain O'Shea was granted a decree nisi with Parnell cited as the co-respondent. Parnell's affair with Mrs O'Shea was well known in closed political circles; but now it was public knowledge, and Gladstone realised the damage that might be inflicted on the cause of Home Rule: as he put it, using Scots dialect, 'It'll na dee'. Or, as he explained in a more expanded form in a secret memorandum on 21 November 1890:

> No man ought to suffer prejudice in his public capacity for any conduct, except such as is known . . . All the matter then, which was put in proof in the O'Shea case, is to be taken as known.

The cause of 'constitutional Home Rule' had to be decided by the free assent of the people also of Great Britain; and the 'Irish demand' had to be pleaded in the House of Commons. In these circumstances, the central point was that:

> Mr Parnell's weight and moral force in Parliament were likely to be impaired or lost by the continuance of his leadership, and that the Liberal constituencies would not, as matter of fact, be available in their unimpaired strength, under that condition, for returning to Parliament friends of the national cause of Ireland.[37]

Gladstone instructed John Morley to let the Irish party know, through one of its members, Justin McCarthy, that Parnell's remaining in the leadership at present would be disastrous. Unfortunately, McCarthy did not inform his party until after Parnell was re-elected Chairman. Gladstone's publication of his letter to McCarthy two days later provoked a crisis for the Gladstonian Liberal–Irish Home Rule alliance, which deepened when, following a party meeting on 15 December 1890, McCarthy led 45 members out of the meeting, leaving Parnell with 28 supporters.

Gladstone saw his hopes of a large Liberal majority in Great Britain, and a clear Nationalist voice from Ireland, dashed. The 1892 general election gave the Liberals and Home Rulers 353 seats, as against 314 Unionists and Liberal Unionists. The Liberals polled better in Scotland and Wales, than in England; but the real anxiety about the result, apart from the low Liberal–Nationalist majority, was Gladstone's acknowledgement of the fact that 'if we had thrown British questions into the shade we should have had no majority at all'.[38] A narrow victory for Home Rule in the Commons would not give the Liberals the moral majority that they needed if they were to try to launch an attack on the House of Lords in the event of their (inevitable) rejection of the Home Rule bill. Nevertheless, Gladstone at first contemplated another attempt in the near future should the Lords reject his bill; but, in the event, the low majority of 34 following the third reading of his bill on 1 September 1893 after 82 sittings and an extended session, made such a return to the fray impracticable. And the Lords' decisive rejection of the Home Rule bill by 419 votes to 41 made it clear that Gladstone's greatest fear (which he expressed in December 1890), that 'the struggle . . . must survive me, cannot be survived by me' would be realised.[39]

After the failure of his second Home Rule bill in 1893 Gladstone simply let his bill drop: he neither went to the country, nor did he resign. And between 1893 and 1906 British parties had other issues to deal with besides Ireland. Already there were signs that the excitement generated by the great controversy of 1886 was abating. Few British Unionists took up the plea of A. V. Dicey (author of *England's Case Against Home Rule*, a brilliant defence of the Union) to spend more time campaigning in Irish constituencies in order to demonstrate that 'the United Kingdom is really a common country' (Dicey also admitted that 'Irish members have sometimes done the Unionists a good deal of harm at English elections').[40] British Unionists, building on the already existing Irish social and economic reform legislation, could, however, come up with a slogan for the British electorate: that of 'killing home rule with kindness'; providing good government as a means of undermining the Nationalist demand for self-government. But this slogan, though attractive, required a great deal more energy than any Unionist administration was prepared to spend on Ireland. It also required more money than either the Liberals or the Unionists were prepared to spend on Ireland. Now that Gladstone was gone, Liberals warned the British public that 'killing home rule' meant that the Unionists would deprive themselves of the opportunity of doing anything useful for the rest of the United Kingdom. Joseph Chamberlain, for his part, countered with the argument that the Liberals in 1893 had proposed giving Ireland autonomy at the cost of two million pounds a year to the British taxpayer.[41]

It was possible to enlist Unionist supporters for the defence of the United Kingdom and the Empire; and it helped shape the modern Conservative image as the patriotic party. But it was less easy to arouse British enthusiasm for spending British money on reforming Ireland out of Home Rule sentiment, especially since the Home Rule movement after 1893 itself showed little sign of life. The result was a declaration of intent – twenty years of resolute government – but little more than piecemeal reforms, some of them, like local government in 1898, extended to Ireland as a means of extricating the Unionist government from the unusual combination of Irish Unionists and Nationalists, who were united in their indignation that Ireland was being overtaxed to the sum of £2,750,000 per annum.[42] An ineffective land act in 1891 was, certainly, followed by a more effective measure in 1896, but the rate of land purchase remained relatively slow. Indeed, it was dissatisfaction with the policy of 'kindness' that encouraged some of the landed elements in the Unionist ranks to get together with the tenants and work out an agreement in 1903 which, within a decade, virtually eliminated landlordism from rural Ireland. The government measure which embodied this agreement (Wyndham's Act) was the produce of local Irish, not British Unionist initiative.

There was another underlying weakness in the policy of killing Home Rule with kindness. This policy moved the British state towards treating people as citizens rather than subjects; and one that would cease to distinguish between 'loyal' and 'disloyal' nationalities in the United Kingdom, since all were now to be treated alike, and as standing (in the eyes of the State) on the same, equal footing. As A. J. Balfour put it, 'in truth I am merely doing my best to prevent them picking each other's pockets and cutting each other's throats'.[43] This, in turn, made nonsense of the Irish Unionists' claim that their loyalty placed a greater claim on the British state. Here, then, was a Unionist government seeming to treat nationalist and Unionist Irishmen alike; indeed, it might raise the nationalist above the Unionist, if this were construed to be in the overall and greater interest of the Kingdom. Further, it might necessitate such a process, since the purpose of killing Home Rule with kindness was to win over nationalists to full allegiance to the state (Unionists, by their own token, were already secure in such loyalties). State patronage placed the British government – a British Unionist government – in the position of neutrality between the contending groups in Ireland;[44] and it is not fanciful to see in this the beginnings of that 'neutrality' that was to become more apparent, and of greater significance, in the climactic years of the Irish Question in British politics, between 1916 and 1923.

The policy of 'kindness' has been most closely associated with Arthur James Balfour, whose aesthetic exterior masked a cold, but clear-sighted, grasp of Irish realities. But a closer study of his Irish career reveals that the Irish Question in British politics could never be lost sight of as precisely that: an Irish issue on the British political scene. No-one was more vehement than Balfour in his contempt for the notion that there was any such thing as Irish nationality; no-one was more certain that the real issue in Ireland was that of the general attack upon property and stability which radical and socialistic elements in the United Kingdom were bent upon.[45] Unionists sought to do just so much to satisfy the British public that Britain was treating Ireland 'justly' (but no more), and was maintaining a firm grip on lawless elements in Ireland (but not falling into the trap of an unreasonable use of force). When Balfour was inclined to suppress nationalist newspapers and even prosecute newsvendors, he was in any case brought up sharply by Salisbury, who reminded him that there was a 'general (English) prejudice about the press'.[46] And while he approved of Wyndham's land purchase act, Balfour was concerned about the fact that the measure might be 'represented as a great gift to the Irish tenants and landlords at the cost of the British taxpayer'; however he accepted that the cabinet was 'clearly of the opinion that in the interests of a great policy minor difficulties must be ignored'.[47]

IV

Balfour would not push an Irish policy beyond the limits he believed that British public would set upon it; but he was prepared to do enough to demonstrate that the United Kingdom was a seamless political garment. The necessity of combining a progressive political image with regard to Ireland, and at the same time showing unflinching determination to keep Ireland in order, was unlikely to go beyond a holding operation. If Ireland could be made to *appear* assimilated into the general British political scene, then this was as good an Irish policy as any, and better than the bitter and divided Gladstonian policy that had split their Liberal opponents. But in 1904–5 the attempts by Sir Anthony MacDonnell, the under-secretary at Dublin Castle, and Lord Dunraven, one of the chief architects of the land settlement of 1903, to extend the policy of cooperation from the economic to the political sphere through a scheme of devolution, revealed that British parties could not always remain in the driving seat when it came to Irish politics. The devolution scheme envisaged the establishment of a central Irish council exercising a specified measure of local autonomy; but its publication on 26 September 1904 aroused Unionist cries of betrayal to its nationalist enemies. If nationalists were always prepared to bite the hand that (Unionists alleged) fed them, then how much worse for British Unionists to feed the hand that bit them. Nothing excited Unionist hatred more than a sense of betrayal, and betrayal at the hands of 'certain members of His Majesty's government' who would 'lightly throw them overboard without regret'.[48] Balfour had a party to lead and a government to keep together; and the MacDonnell scheme could no more be considered on its merits, whatever they might be, than any other Irish policy. This was especially the case when, after 1903, he had lost five cabinet ministers on the issue of free trade versus tariff reform. No government could afford to burden itself with another divisive and contentious issue; but Balfour's decision not to publish the correspondence relating to the issue on the grounds that civil servants' anonymity must be protected only provoked further suspicions that more serious measures had been contemplated.[49]

But the affair went deeper than this. The Unionist Party had toyed with a scheme that was less than maintaining the Union pure and simple; within a few years a Liberal government was to consider a scheme that was less than Home Rule, with equally troublesome results, as the nationalists united to denounce this reneging on the Liberal commitment to Irish self-government.

Conciliation was, for the Unionists, and then the Liberals, an uneasy policy, if it were pushed to any appreciable lengths: land reform, even local government reform, congested districts boards, measures for the improvement of Irish agriculture were all very well. But anything that smacked of constitutional conciliation was anathema to Irish Unionist and Nationalist alike. The appointment of Walter Long, a convinced Unionist and fervent admirer of the Irish Unionists, as Irish Chief Secretary in 1905 was a sign of the growing Irish Unionist influence on the party, an influence that was not broken until 1916. The strength of Irish Unionist 'betrayal' feeling provoked Balfour into demonstrating that they were not in any danger of being 'gratuitously abandoned', and was one of the factors which prevented him from asking for a mid-term dissolution. It also inspired the organisation of the Ulster Unionist Council in July 1905, a body which subsumed all shades of Unionist opinion in Ulster, including Liberal Unionists, who would now hold a stronger position in British as well as Irish political circles. For many good political reasons it was easier for the British Unionist Party and its Irish allies to adopt an intransigent attitude to the Irish Question, and to forsake the sombre, but considered Unionism of Lord Salisbury's era for a new, raucous and bitter attacking style.

The British political system is one that embraces its main parties in a common political culture: moderation provokes moderation, and a more strident note finds an echo. The Unionist party and the Liberals had confronted each other over Home Rule in 1886; but after 1892 the Unionists' gradual retreat from its unusually ideological position was matched by a Liberal retreat from the high peaks of Gladstonian commitment to Ireland. There was the general nervousness that the British electorate did not want their parties to spend too much time on Irish issues; and there was the feeling among the Liberals in particular that a lower profile on Home Rule might encourage the return of the Liberal Unionists to the fold, and would in any case free the party from its central identification with Home Rule, all the more essential in an imperially-minded age. There was even the fear that Home Rule might exclude the party from office permanently. Even in 1886 it seemed that the British

Liberal opinion supported Home Rule less out of sympathy to Ireland than out of loyalty to Gladstone. In 1903 the Liberal–Home Rulers alliance stood on the threshold of a major transformation.

But the Unionist crisis over devolution was, given the nature of the British party system, a crisis also for the Liberals. The Unionist retreat from devolution naturally encouraged those elements in the Irish Parliamentary Party, represented by John Dillon, who opposed concessions from the Unionists on the grounds that they were a plot to weaken Home Rule sentiment in Ireland, and who believed that the old Westminster-centred policy of depending upon the Liberal government to pass Home Rule over the heads of any opposition in Ireland was (if short-sighted) at least a policy on which the party could be kept together – and party unity was as important to the Home Rulers as to anyone else. But party loyalty was of a very different character in Ireland than in England. In England party loyalty did not involve the consolidation of the party's support to the exclusion of large sections of the English people, or even Scottish or Welsh people. In Ireland 'unity' meant the bringing together of those who belonged together, as the Afrikaaner Nationalists put it, and the abandonment of any policies that might be calculated to woo Unionist opinion. There were to be sure limits beyond which Unionist opinion could not be wooed; but any likelihood of the 'conference plus business' mood that had produced the 1903 Land Conference was destroyed by the return of Parnellite tactics.

The Liberal Party entered upon government in 1906 with a massive parliamentary majority and the option of leaving Home Rule in abeyance, an option which it showed every sign of exercising. Like the Unionists after 1900, the Liberals were more willing to consider other ways forward in Irish policy, for their mood naturally matched that of the Unionists who had showed a willingness to move away from the crisis-ridden atmosphere of Home Rule versus Union. Campbell Bannerman's administration declared that it would consider the granting of 'local powers and removing topics from the British Parliament, while retaining its ultimate control'[50] but it contained some members who stipulated

45

that there should be no new Home Rule bill. The party saw more advantage in applying social and economic reforms to the United Kingdom as a whole, and gradualism in all things Irish. The Irish Parliamentary Party had little choice but to accept this; and anyway there was nothing too inconsistent in accepting what the government had to offer, since the party had, from the earliest times, lived and indeed thrived on the winning of real and tangible concessions, on land, on education, while waiting for the great day of freedom to dawn.

But the new atmosphere, already damaged by the MacDonnell devolution crisis for the Unionists, was further damaged by a similar controversy for the Liberals. The new Liberal government was regarded by some Unionists as 'a majority of groups held together by the slenderest of threads'[51] and such a government, containing diverse radical and Whiggish groups, must stress party unity. Massive majorities were not a guarantee of political stability in a party, and might indeed work to the opposite effect, allowing dissident elements to have their say with impunity. Any crisis for the party was a real one; and in 1906–7 the Liberals met a problem similar to that which troubled the Unionists in 1904. The government introduced an Irish Councils Bill which would give Irish people a fuller share in the government of Ireland, while not going as far as Home Rule; there would be an increased local participation in, and some degree of responsibility for, certain parochial Irish and administrative affairs. The bill could be regarded as either a substitute for Home Rule, or as a step towards it; but ambiguity, a useful tool in British politics, held dangers for the Irish nationalists, especially when the government failed to consult them until the bill's later stages. This raised the hopes of John Redmond and his party, only to dash them when the bill's moderate provisions were revealed. Now it was the nationalists' turn to cry betrayal; and with the party in danger of splitting over the issue, Redmond had little choice but to condemn it out of hand.

The consequences of this for the Liberal Party were profound; profound indeed for the whole Irish Question in British politics. The moves towards a sort of unofficial bipartisanship between 1900 and 1906, undermined by the MacDonnell incident, were now destroyed by the Irish Councils Bill affair. In any case, it was axiomatic that bipartisanship could only work if both major British parties agreed to work it: unilateral bipartisanship was (to say the least) a contradiction in terms. But the 1906–7 controversy left the Liberals with no alternative Irish policy save that of the full measure of Gladstonian Home Rule, and moreover, Gladstonian in its refusal to allow any special recognition of the Ulster problem.

V

By 1908, then, the wheel of the Irish Question in British politics had turned full circle; and like many political motions – perhaps most – had come back to rest in the same position. For it is misleading to think that political parties, which are the makers of what political scientists like to call 'political systems' are always or even mainly masters of their own destiny. Their short-term political needs and the logic of their political rhetoric often determined their course of action. When the Unionists and the Liberals confronted the consequences of their own tactics and party political programmes on Ireland in 1905 and 1908 they could do nothing other than shoulder the burdens of 1886 once again.

The British perception of what constituted the Irish Question had a decisive impact on Ireland – and, in turn, on the nature of the Irish Question in British politics. Between 1868 and 1908 landlordism in Ireland had been dismantled, religious grievances met, a Roman Catholic educational system established at all levels, local government made democratic, the franchise extended, and in short, Ireland handed over to the priest and the farmer. But not yet to the Home Rulers, who never lost sight of the attractiveness of replacing a Protestant ascendancy by a Roman Catholic or Nationalist one. The elimination of social and economic grievances (though not of course all of them, which was beyond the scope of nineteenth and probably twentieth-century political action anyway) did not free British political parties from the Irish Question; on the contrary, the elimination of these important grievances only simplified the question in a drastic and dangerous way, and left the Liberals and Unionists with less, not more, room for manoeuvre, as their 1905 and 1908 crises demonstrated. This room for manoeuvre was further limited by the increased sectarian atmosphere of Irish politics in the new century, and by the emergence of the Irish, and especially Ulster Unionists as a coherent and well-organised force ranged in bitter opposition to Irish Home Rule, a predicament that had not troubled Gladstone in 1886, when Home Rule came, as Unionists put it, like a thief in the night. Now, after the 1906 general election, Irish Unionists made up about 1 in 8 of the entire Unionist party's parliamentary membership: a considerable increase in the strength, and therefore the influence, of Irish Unionism, if a somewhat fortuitous one. By 1908 the British political parties could not escape from the logic of their political policies as well as their political beliefs; the new atmosphere of British domestic politics after 1908 ensured that they would not want to do so, even if they could.

2

A QUESTION OF PARTISANSHIP, 1909–22: BRITISH PARTY POLITICS, THE GREAT WAR AND IRELAND

I

In 1909 the Liberal and Unionist Parties found themselves in the most irreconcilable political disagreement of their modern political history. This was inspired by a mixture of political issues and political tactics; and the Irish Question was soon gathered up into this mixture, so much that it was quite inseparable from it. For there is a tendency to see Ireland as invading British political space yet again, as disrupting the even tenor of British political ways, as introducing into British politics the savage disagreements characteristic of politics in Ireland. Yet Ireland alone could not have provoked this, despite the fact that the political parties found themselves once again left with Home Rule versus Union as an integral part of their political descriptions. In November 1906 Austen Chamberlain declared that 'just now, for an Englishman, at any rate, a speech on Home Rule is like flogging a dead horse'.[1] The movement of Ireland to the centre of the political stage involved its recognition by the major parties as a public issue essential to the outcome of their party battle.

This battle, between 1909 and 1911, was joined on constitutional grounds; for, despite the reform bills from 1832 until 1884, Britain had not, contrary to the traditional accounts, moved easily from oligarchy to democracy; indeed, she had not moved to democracy at all, but to a mixture of elite and popular politics. The parties were aware of the opportunities and disadvantages of a new reform bill, of tackling plural voting, or women's suffrage; and this detailed speculation was part of the broader question of the distribution and wielding of political power in Britain. Unionists believed firmly that the Liberal government which won power in 1906 was a government hardly fit to be trusted with the task of running a great nation and a great empire; had not sections of the party supported the Boers, and did they still not lend a sympathetic ear to the Irish Nationalists? A. J. Balfour saw the Irish Question as one of Unionism arrayed not only against Irish Home Rulers, but against the whole army of those who would be king: socialists, anarchists, radicals, those who had rioted in central London in 1884–86, whose rising power was revealed in the election of 59 Labour MPs to the House of Commons in 1906, and some of whom at least were ensconced in the Liberal cabinet. Such enemies could only be stopped by a resolute Unionist rearguard action, using the House of Lords as the means of thwarting and frustrating the government's legislative programme. 'There has certainly never been a period in our history', Balfour confided to Lord Lansdowne, 'in which the House of Lords would be called upon to play a part at once so important, so delicate, and so difficult'.[2] Any cabinet with Lloyd George and Winston Churchill among its number could not be trusted to govern in the spirit of the British constitution, to respect property, to preserve liberty, those twin bastions of the constitutional system since 1688. Hence the outrage of the Unionist Party at Lloyd George's 'People's Budget' of 1909, which included a proposal to tax the profits accruing from the ownership of land, for land was the Englishman's birthright and inheritance, and had not been subject to government depredations since the seventeenth century.

Unionist rhetoric in the prewar Home Rule crisis has been compared to that of the seventeenth century; but this can be applied also to the crisis over the People's Budget, and the Liberals responded in kind by comparing the Unionist opposition to the land tax to the 'Norman Yoke' first fastened on free Saxons in 1066, and then fastened upon them again in the time of Charles I. Irish issues were not at all alien to this cacaphony of political voices. But of course rhetoric was not enough. The party battle, and the prospects of the Unionists dividing the Liberals among themselves, giving their supporters a good rallying cry, and putting the government in the most difficult position possible contributed to the general crisis. Some Unionists believed – quite rightly – that not all Liberals were happy to be seen as pro Home Rule. And the role of Ireland in the party battle was sharpened by the government's own handling of the budget issue in relation to the support, or potential support, of the Irish Parliamentary Party.

Lloyd George's budget was not framed to provoke the House of Lords, for the Liberals were doubtful about the popular appeal of a campaign against the upper house; and not all Liberals wanted to handle the Lords roughly anyway: A. J. Balfour speculated that many Liberals would be secretly grateful for the moderating influence of the Lords on the more radical wing of the Liberal Party; and he believed that if the Lords used 'caution and tact', then no harm would be done.[3] The upper house had shown itself willing in 1907 to reform its own composition to render the use of its powers less contentious. Balfour showed no interest in this approach, even though it would have blunted Liberal criticism; and the parties were set on a course of confrontation.

The Liberal budget was not a piece of provocation; it was something more politically useful: a move that ensured that the government could not lose, whatever happened. The government needed to raise extra money, and the policy of taxing unearned income from land was a means of realising revenue: but if the Lords were to reject the budget, then they would strengthen the case against themselves. Yet the budget was bound to be a highly contentious issue; and one open to two main charges, one of them tactical, the other a matter of principal. Tactically, it could be alleged that the Liberals were 'tacking', that is using a financial measure as a vehicle for effecting a policy of wealth redistribution and social levelling. And its land tax, its licensing duties, and its increased death duties represented a 'socialistic' assault on long cherished British beliefs (and not only Conservative beliefs). The Unionists, in Lords and Commons, resolved to resist the budget; and as Lloyd George and Winston Churchill's

provocative speeches began to have an effect, compromise became more difficult. Balfour let it be known that he would resign
if the Peers did not reject the measure. The budget passed the
Commons on 4 November and was defeated in the Lords on 30
November. Lloyd George had campaigned for a public verdict on
the People's Budget; the Lords rejected it on the grounds that the
people must be allowed to judge. There was now no other
possibility but to go to the country and make the finance bill a
general election issue.

The general election of January 1910 resulted in a narrow
victory for the government which now came unfortunately near
to depending on an Irish vote on a central British constitutional
matter;[4] and its authority was damaged by its own mishandling
of the Irish over the question of seeking guarantees from the king
that he would create enough peers if necessary to ensure the
budget's passage through the Lords, and over the budget tax on
whiskey.

Asquith had declared in December 1909 that his party was
ready again to take up Home Rule, and that 'in the new house
of commons the hands of a Liberal government and of a Liberal
majority will be entirely free'.[5] But the Irish Parliamentary Party,
prodded by John Dillon, wished to drive a hard bargain with the
Liberals and ensure the passage of any future Home Rule bill, by
means of guarantees and the limitation of the Lords veto on
Commons' legislation. When this was publicly stated by Redmond in Dublin on 10 February 1910, London was thrown into
crisis, and some Liberals expected the government to fall within
a matter of weeks. Sir Edward Grey was adamant that reform of
the Lords meant reform of its composition, not its powers, and
he was particularly anxious to free the government from any
suspicion that it would have to rely on Irish votes; and Asquith's
uncertain leadership enabled Grey's views to gather strength,
until Lloyd George rallied the more radical wing of the cabinet.
Now Lloyd George stated that the government would not touch
the budget until the necessary veto resolutions had been promul-
gated. 'This', wrote Austen Chamberlain, 'is the first surrender to
the Irish and other malcontents'.[6]

Unionist discontent was fuelled by the reflection that the

government had perhaps nearly fallen over the veto versus composition question. But the Irish knew that they could not push matters to the proof; and that if they deserted the government over the budget controversy, then they forfeited Home Rule. The crisis was resolved when the government finally agreed to 'contingent guarantees' from the king that would ensure the passage of the government's House of Lords legislation; at the same time they stood firm over the budget's whiskey tax, which Redmond and the Irish objected to, knowing that Redmond would not upset the government when he had his main objective, the reduction of the Lords' powers, in his hand. This would enable the Liberals to pose as firm opponents of a 'discreditable transaction' with the Irish, that is of amending the budget in return for Irish support of the government's policies. At least, this was how the Liberals liked to see it; but the Unionist opposition viewed the matter otherwise. Whiskey taxes had been defended by the Liberals, certainly; but the constitution, they alleged, had been put up for sale to the Irish, with Lloyd George, Churchill and their ilk acting as the auctioneers. Asquith had bought the Irish vote for his budget; the price he paid was 'the dignity of his office, and of all the great traditions which he, of all men, ought to uphold'. The Liberals had behaved like a revolutionary gang; they had broken the rules of the constitution; they were even accused in May 1910 of killing the king, who died, Unionists alleged, as a result of the government's unscrupulous behaviour. Following the death of the king and the accession of George V, Asquith and Balfour resorted to the expedient of a constitutional conference to seek accommodation on the great issues of the day: including, hopefully, Home Rule. Here was an attempt at 'bipartisanship'; but this fell far short of Lloyd George's notion of a coalition of 'half a dozen first rate men' who might trade like for like: or Home Rule for a big navy and a commission on tariffs.[7] Both party leaders were, after all, party leaders; and there was a limit to Asquith's compliance, and a greater limit to Balfour's capacity to compromise, for his position in the Unionist Party was vulnerable. In any case Unionists would not agree to a reform of the Lords unless they were certain that the upper house would retain the power to resist a Commons majority that might be used to pass legislation forged as a result of a 'corrupt bargain'. Compromise was impossible where both parties had little to gain from it, and much to lose; and Asquith would have found it difficult to justify abandoning his party's high ground on the Lords question, just as Balfour could not compromise on a settlement that left his party bereft of its strongest unifying force: opposition to Irish Home Rule and defence of the Union.

This is not to say that the British public at large was unreservedly cheering on their main political parties as they became locked in battle over the Lords, and then the Home Rule, issue. There was sympathy for Unionist Ulster, but also, especially among the more sophisticated opinion makers, plenty of evidence of the desire for a settlement, perhaps for some kind of federal reorganisation of the United Kingdom that would accommodate the hopes of Irish nationalists and the fears of Ulster Unionists alike. But this only made life more difficult for the party leaders; and especially for the Unionists, who in August 1911 suffered the humiliation of defeat on the parliament act, which deprived the upper house of its veto on Commons legislation. The Unionists' unity – a unity based on opposition to Home Rule – would be jeopardised by any possibility of a settlement that stopped short of the whole demand, for there were those in the party who might want to draw back from the total commitment to Union, and settle for something less: perhaps some form of special treatment for Protestant Ulster. Liberals were apparently united behind their leader and his Irish allies; but the uneasy relationship with Redmond and his party was made more troublesome by the feeling among some Liberals that the party had really done – or at least promised – enough for Ireland, and that some compromise might be necessary: clipping the wings of the Lords was one thing, but helping Redmond to feather his nest was quite another. Liberal doubts were evident in the general elections of January and December 1910, when 9 of the 16 ministers who issued addresses made no reference to Home Rule, and only 84 out of 272 successful Liberal candidates mentioned it in the December campaign.[8] There was a feeling that the party was engaged in controversies that ought to have been settled long ago. Thus in both parties there were different degrees of commitment to the Irish Question, and the consequent danger of party splits, faction and loss of morale; and also the risk of adverse reaction from the Liberals' and Unionists' Irish allies, for Redmond on the one hand, and Carson and Sir James Craig on the other, were ever vigilant for signs of reticence or backsliding on the part of their British advocates.

This helps explain the way in which the main British political parties drifted into an ever worsening crisis after the introduction of the third Home Rule bill in April 1912. It is significant that no sooner was the bill tabled, than there were proposals for a compromise: the Liberal member, Agar-Robartes, moved an amendment to exclude from the bill the counties of Armagh, Antrim, Down and Londonderry. This placed the Unionist opposition in some difficulty. Their new leader, Andrew Bonar Law, was concerned mainly with the fate of Unionist Ulster, and had little understanding of the Protestants in the rest of Ireland; but there were those in the party like Walter Long, who warned that they would not abandon the Unionists of the south and west of Ireland, and who also wished to defend the Union in the interests of England and the whole kingdom.[9] The Unionists' dilemma was resolved by that equally felt difficulty which the Agar-Robartes amendment posed to the Liberals; for it to pass would require the Liberals to break ranks over Home Rule and risk their alliance with Redmond; and Redmond for his part feared above all that his allies would indeed in the end confront him with some such proposal that he would find difficult to refuse. It was easier all round to play the tactical game: to appear reasonable, the Unionists accepted the amendment, knowing it would be defeated. The government for its part was not yet ready to admit that the time for compromise had come, especially when it might destroy its unity and parliamentary strength. Its determination to proceed with the bill, unamended, was reinforced by Redmond's assurances that the Ulster Unionists' opposition to Home Rule – an opposition which quickly took on a military form as well as militant language – was merely a bluff: a 'phenomenon of hysteria'.[10]

The world of politics is an uncertain one; and it is for that reason that politicians like to grasp hold of such certainties as are available. It was certain that to compromise, or to compromise too soon, would raise as many difficulties as it would solve; yet both parties had to make some effort at appearing reasonable in the eyes of a British public which, bombarded as it was with propaganda on behalf of Unionists and nationalists alike, was regarded by both British parties as the unknown factor that might in the end prove important, if not decisive. Unionists' hopes that they would win an election if they could only force the government to it were tempered by doubts about the popularity of the Irish issue with the average voter. Liberals were aware of the contradictions of their position, as a party whose Nonconformist roots hardly sat easily with the policy of coercing Ulster Protestants for the benefit of Irish Roman Catholics, and whose principles rendered it difficult to contemplate using military force to subdue a minority in Ireland. Liberal offers to allow certain Ulster counties a temporary 'opting out' of the jurisdiction of an all-Ireland parliament marked a compromise between its political necessities (to maintain party unity and the nationalist alliance) and the need to demonstrate to the British public that it was not wholly deaf to the cries of Ulster Unionists. Unionist tactics were dictated by the need to avoid a split between those who saw Ulster as the prime target, those who still hoped to defend the Union outright and those who sought a general federal settlement of the whole constitutional question; and the need to appear reasonable in the eyes of the general public, by pressing the government to hold an election on the Home Rule bill and thus submit it to the final will of the electorate. But the government could no more concede an election than the opposition could accept a compromise on the Union.

The Unionist concentration on Ulster was, therefore, the consequence of their desire to appear 'moderate and reasonable' in the eyes of British public opinion.[11] But if the government were to concede on 'county option' then it must also appear 'firm', and show its readiness to take precautionary moves. The 'Curragh incident' in March 1914, when certain officers of the 3rd Cavalry Brigade took advantage of administrative confusion to declare their refusal to march north in the event of trouble or conflict with the Ulster Unionists, ended the possibility of 'firmness'. The government's embarrassment reinforced the opposition's belief that Asquith must now submit to a dissolution and an election; it also, however, left the government with no alternative but to press on with its Home Rule bill, if only to demonstrate that it would not be deflected by unrest in the army. Asquith dared hope that the Curragh incident would cost the Unionists support among moderate British opinion.[12] These contradictory pressures – between the government's and the opposition's desire to appear reasonable before the British public, and yet keep their parties together and sustain their morale on the great issue of the day – explains both their agreement to enter the Buckingham Palace conference in July 1914 to see if compromise could be reached, and the impossibility of reaching compromise. When the conference broke down on the question of defining the area of Ulster to be excluded (let alone the question of a time limit on exclusion) the Unionists felt that they had emerged with credit: 'we are now in a splendid position to say that for the sake of peace we have explored a certain path to the utmost and found it led nowhere'.[13]

It was easier for both parties, caught in their internal dilemma and their external relationship with the British electorate, to chose paths which indeed led 'nowhere'; but this increased the chances of what Austen Chamberlain feared most, 'not civil war ... but anarchy'.[14] There were those in the Unionist Party who saw civil war, if not anarchy, as preferable to the surrender to those in the government who stood for the corruption and decadence of British political life: the Liberal plutocracy, the philistine press, the anti-imperialists. Even if party unity had not tied Bonar Law's hands, and inhibited him from moving towards what he really desired – a settlement based on the exclusion of Ulster – these forces in his party would have threatened the basis of the whole British political and constitutional system if any such compromise were suggested. Certainties were, in the end, the best guide for the politician; and certainties must be pursued even if the whole United Kingdom were to continue on its very uncertain path in the summer of 1914. Only a major shift in British politics, and a realignment of the parties, could prepare the way for a resolution of the Irish Question on the basis of special treatment for Unionist Ulster, adumbrated in the debates and conferences of 1913 and 1914. This realignment was eventually rendered possible by the pressures of the Great War; but it could not be created merely by ideas of coalitions, bipartisanship or constitutional conferences: politics does not always work on the principle of rationality.

The last stage of the crisis over the third Home Rule bill demonstrated the intractability of the party battle. The Unionists on 30 August offered to defer controversial domestic quarrels in the interests of a united war effort; but they insisted that this should be conditional on the postponement of the Home Rule bill (and the bill for the disestablishment of the Church of Wales) in their present form. The government was unwilling to have the international crisis used to the disadvantage of its two major policies, and it responded by placing the Home Rule bill on the statute book, but suspending its operation for six months, or until the end of the war, whichever should be shorter. Asquith also promised an amending bill providing for the (unspecified) exclusion of Ulster. The Unionists were outraged at this sleight of hand, as they saw it; some even considered using the Lords to obstruct it, or a parliamentary filibuster. But Law and Lansdowne persuaded the party that this would only rebound on their own heads. A protest meeting was held at the Carlton Club and a mass withdrawal of the party from the Commons satisfied Unionist anger. But at least the opposition agreed to a party truce, and to a formal arrangement whereby vacant seats would not be contested at by-elections, providing, as Law put it, there was no 'jiggery-pokery' over Irish Home Rule and Welsh disestablishment.[15]

II

Within less than a year the Unionists found themselves in a coalition with their hated Liberal enemies. This was not the inevitable outcome of the Unionist desire to show that they were responsible and patriotic supporters of the war effort: Unionists were perfectly sure that they were patriots anyway. It was better to leave the conduct of the war to the government, especially when that conduct only added further proof to the Unionist contention that the Liberals were unfit to govern. But Unionists found it impossible to resist Asquith's offer in May 1915, after a series of failures on both the military and organisational fronts, of a coalition government. There was much of mutual self-interest to be gained, quite apart from the real necessity of a more vigorous prosecution of the war. Bonar Law did not relish the prospect of forming a Unionist administration, since his own party was deeply divided on so many issues, including the difficult one of compulsory national service; Asquith, far from ceding power to his opponents, would harness them to his government, and proceed with a strengthened hand (and, hopefully, silence criticism of his style). Asquith was prepared to meet Unionist demands, including the removal of Lord Haldane, the demotion of Churchill and the placing of Lloyd George in the Ministry of Munitions. The Liberals kept the main government posts; Unionist backbenchers continued to sit as the opposition. And, for Ireland, there was one significant pointer: Sir Edward Carson, leader of Unionist resistance to Home Rule in the prewar crisis, became Attorney General; Redmond was offered, but refused, an official post. This was not meant as a blow to the cause of Home Rule; but it was an indication that Home Rule was secondary to the major consideration, that of winning the war. Any slight to nationalist Ireland was not only unintentional: it was unimportant in the light of larger events.

Still, at least the appointment of Augustine Birrell to the Irish chief secretaryship showed that a Home Ruler still sat in the seat of power when it came to administering Ireland; but the question about the precise nature of the coalition's Irish policy was not yet put to the test. That test came when at Easter, 1916, the Irish Republican Brotherhood, and other separatist groups, launched an uprising on a startled and unprepared British – and Irish – nation. The rising was suppressed and its leaders executed by the military, which satisfied Unionists; but Asquith made a visit to Ireland – 'a very curious experience' – and on his return announced that he had authorised Lloyd George to open fresh talks with Irish Nationalist and Unionist spokesmen. Lloyd George hoped to use the sense of emergency, and the Irish

Parliamentary Party's condemnation of the rising, to rush a settlement through, and he quickly secured a measure of agreement between Redmond and Carson. This is not surprising, for, apart from Lloyd George's supreme gifts as a negotiator, Carson was willing to place the Empire's welfare above that of his Unionism, and Redmond needed a Dublin parliament, for already his hold on the country had been weakened by General Maxwell's firing squads. Lloyd George offered the immediate establishment of Home Rule with the exclusion of the six counties which now form Northern Ireland. Lloyd George's methods were not without danger; his failure to disclose the progress of the negotiations until he had already deeply committed himself and (Redmond and Carson believed) the government, shocked the coalition Unionists; and Lloyd George allowed a necessary ambiguity over the question of the permanency, or otherwise, of partition, to lodge in the minds of the Irish spokesmen.

But this did not destroy his settlement; the problem was not ambiguity, which Redmond for his part was willing to put up with as a price for an immediate prospect of power; the difficulty lay with those Unionists in the cabinet, led by Walter Long, whose opposition to Irish Home Rule had not abated since 1914. Lord Selborne, who had supported a federal solution in the prewar crisis, now protested at the prospect of immediate and unconditional self-government for an Ireland seething, he believed, with disaffection. Lord Lansdowne, a prominent southern Irish Unionist and landlord, formed the third chief opponent of the Lloyd George plan. On 27 June they argued that Home Rule would only be regarded as a surrender to force. Yet they had to choose their ground carefully, for the prospect of an emergency settlement was one that received widespread support in the British press; and a survey of Unionist opinion in the constituencies commissioned by Bonar Law revealed that the vast bulk of those canvassed was in favour of a settlement, providing Ulster's position was not compromised thereby. The Unionists in the cabinet concentrated their fire on the ambiguous part of the plan, the permanent or temporary nature of Ulster's exclusion from the Home Rule bill, and they demanded a reduction in the number of Irish MPs sitting at Westminister. They also pressed for a firmer law and order policy, which was only calculated to undermine Redmond's authority in a Dublin executive. Lloyd George and Asquith might have campaigned for the settlement, Lloyd George might have resigned. But to push matters thus far would be to risk the break-up of the government and perhaps irreparably damage the war effort. And Law began to receive contradictory responses from outside, for in June and July he was bombarded with letters and telegrams from people protesting that the Home Rule plan was a 'breach of the party truce', a 'most dangerous expedient at a most critical time'. It was easier to whittle down the terms of the settlement than to risk the destruction of the cabinet. And, as in 1914, it was better in the short term at least to maintain party, and this time also coalition, unity than to risk it as the price of an Irish settlement. British political conditions dictated the terms which Asquith forced on Redmond, and that Redmond could not accept; and the very lack of a settlement kept the government, and the Unionist Party, together.[16]

There was no such thing, therefore, as a coalition Irish policy, except the necessity not to have one. But 1916 was a decisive year; the year after which political change, or even revolution, brought about by the pressures of total war, undermined the stability of some of the apparently most enduring political structures of the prewar era. The United Kingdom escaped most of these repercussions; but even here there were consequences which politicians had to face up to. It is doubtful if anyone cared all that much about the challenge offered to the Irish Parliamentary Party by the rising attraction of Sinn Fein. It was rather that Ireland was becoming increasingly an international problem, as Britain's allies in the Empire, and her potential ally, the United States, had to be convinced that the British government was doing all it reasonably could to put matters right so that the war effort would not suffer. In March 1917 the war cabinet at last began to cast round for an Irish policy, with Bonar Law declaring that, in spite of the risks, 'it is worthwhile for us, on our own responsibility, in some way or another to make another attempt'. This vague gesture was given more conviction by the entry of the

United States into the war in April. And at last, on 16 May 1917, Lloyd George outlined the government's proposals: an offer of Home Rule, with the exclusion of the six north-eastern counties, as in 1916; or a 'Convention of Irishmen of all parties for the purpose of producing a scheme of Irish self-government'.

This was a master stroke of improvisation: if any Irish party refused to participate, they would appear unreasonable in the eyes of the world; if they cooperated then Britain would be left alone to get on with the war. As Geoffrey Dawson put it, 'every day it sits is a day gained'.[17] The Irish Convention did sit and gained many days for Britain, between its inaugural meeting on 25 July 1917 and its final report in April of the following year. But much time was lost for the Irish Parliamentary Party, whose rival, Sinn Fein, did not enter the convention and so were not compromised by the process of bargaining that produced a measure of agreement between the main body of southern Unionists and Irish Home Rulers, but left the Ulster Question unresolved. But by now the demands of British politics began to push events in a new, and more ominous direction. The government had first introduced limited conscription for Great Britain, but not for Ireland, in March 1916; now, as the flow of volunteers for the British army dwindled, and the German offensive of March 1918 necessitated another compulsory demand on British manpower, public opinion and the British parties naturally looked to Ireland as a source of recruits to the colours. Lloyd George had misgivings about applying any new measure of conscription to Ireland; but it was difficult to resist the tide of public and political opinion. However, he was able to push his government nearer to a recognition of the need for some kind of settlement of the Irish Question by declaring that, while it was impossible to ask 'our people to make sacrifices . . . and leave the Irish at home out', nevertheless, whatever the outcome of the Irish Convention, he would take up the responsibility for producing a new Home Rule bill and passing it into law.

Once against British Unionists had to take stock of their commitment to Ireland; and even to Unionist Ulster. They could hardly stand in the way of Home Rule if it were a real and immediate war necessity, especially if it were to bring Irish conscription nearer. And the party's grip on the Union was further loosened by a split in the southern Unionist ranks, when some of the moderate elements, led by Lord Midleton, declared themselves willing to cooperate with Nationalists in a Home Rule parliament for the whole of Ireland. This attitude contrasted unfavourably with that of the Ulster Unionists who stood firm in the Irish Convention against any concession to Dublin rule, and for the first time British Unionists were driven to make some criticisms of Ulster Unionist lack of 'patriotism', an accusation that was angrily repudiated.[18] No-one would coerce Ulster into an all-Ireland polity; but there were hopes that she might be persuaded to accept some form of compromise (which might involve an all-Ireland polity).

The government established an Irish Committee to draft a Home Rule bill while it braced itself for the conscription crisis; but if it proved difficult to draw up a bill that would satisfy all the parties in Ireland, it was hardly any easier to draft one that would satisfy all the parties in Britain either. Some Unionists now favoured a federal solution, which would fit Ireland and Ulster into a reorganised United Kingdom, and thus deprive Ulster of her main argument against Home Rule – that it was a special form of treatment for Ireland, at variance with the practice of the rest of the kingdom. But others, like Lord Curzon and A. J. Balfour, objected strongly, declaring that Great Britain was not ready for such a radical constitutional change, and that they could not consent to 'pull up the British constitution by the roots.[19] Very quickly the Irish Committee became involved in a bewildering array of legal and administrative questions: the compatibility of Home Rule with federalism; the role of the Post Office, the question of customs, trade marks, the judiciary. Long believed that federalism would win an easier passage through the Commons; but the committee also had to acknowledge that 'as a preliminary to proceeding with the Government policy either in respect to conscription or of the grant of self-government to Ireland it was first necessary that the new Irish Administration should restore respect for government, enforce the law and, above all, put down with a stern hand the Irish-German conspiracy which appears to be widespread in Ireland'.[20] Small wonder that one member of the committee asked to be relieved of attendance as he thought the committee was 'ploughing the sands'. And even those observers most sympathetic to an Irish settlement admitted that Ireland would have to be governed 'in the way which had always suited it best':[21] strong military measures.

And yet matters could not go back to 1914. A few days before the armistice of 11 November 1918 there was yet another embarrassing debate on the Irish Question in the Commons. On 22 November Professor W. G. S. Adams, one of Lloyd George's confidential advisers, was requested to prepare a memorandum on the 'Policy of the Government with regard to Home Rule' for circulation to ministers to assist them in their speeches in the forthcoming general election which the coalition would fight under Lloyd George. Adams' memorandum began by asserting that:

> The Government, despite the heavy pressure of War Policy and Administration have earnestly desired and sought to effect a settlement of the Irish question. They have made it plain that a settlement was a matter of great importance for the sake of good feeling between Great Britain and Ireland as well as on Imperial and International grounds.

Adams concluded that the government had further defined its policy in its election manifesto, signed by Lloyd George and Bonar Law:

> Namely, that 'it is one of the first obligations of British statesmanship to explore all practical paths towards a settlement of this grave and difficult question on the basis of self- government. But there are two paths which are closed – the one leading to complete severance of Ireland from the British Empire, and the other to the forcible submission of the six counties of Ulster to a Home Rule parliament against their will.[22]

By the end of the war, Unionism was no longer able in principle to defend the Union intact; the question was whether or not the Unionist Party could discover a means of modifying the Union that would meet the exigencies of the Irish situation, satisfy the British public that the party was not die-hard over this issue, and – above all – keep the party from falling out yet again over the precise nature of any Irish settlement that might be proposed. Coalition had frustrated an Irish solution in 1916; but now coalition might well help to produce one as Lloyd George fought and won his coupon election in December 1918, and formed his new Liberal, Unionist and (in small degree) Labour government. Bonar Law warned his party in 1917 that it was 'looking into a fog', and that moderate Unionism and Liberalism must combine to defeat the threat of militant labour.[23] Now that a 'moderate' combination was achieved, the Unionist Party must do its best for the popular leader of the country, David Lloyd George.

War and now an extension of coalition modified Unionist attitudes to the Union; but it had an equally significant impact on Liberalism. The war opened up a deep and lasting gap between Liberals and Irish nationalism. When the Liberal government placed its Home Rule bill on the statute book in September 1914, this was greeted with vociferous demonstrations of welcome in Westminister and Ireland alike. But this response was based on the expectation that the war would be short, and that Home Rule was within John Redmond's grasp; when Asquith and Lloyd George retreated from the proposed Irish settlement in 1916 Redmond swore never to deal with Lloyd George again. In fact Redmond was obliged to deal with him, or at least to enter into the negotiations which Lloyd George's Irish Convention necessitated. But 1916 really marked the end of the relationship between the Liberals and the Irish Parliamentary Party forged by Gladstone and Parnell in 1886. This alliance had brought benefits to Ireland, but probably not to the Liberal Party; any remote possibility that it might be renewed in some form, however attenuated, was ended by the general election of 1918 which saw the triumph of Sinn Fein, and the abstention of Sinn Fein's 73 MPs from parliament. This, however, removed a complicating factor from the British political scene; and it suited the coalition's belief that there must be all-party solutions to the problems of the postwar world. This would have an impact on Irish policy; and an even greater influence was the recognition that there were problems as great as Ireland, or greater, in the new and dangerous 'fog'.

III

For the moment, the government could claim that it must maintain law and order in Ireland in the face of a recrudescence of the physical force tradition now represented by the Irish Volunteers (soon to be generally known as the Irish Republican Army); and besides the inevitable preoccupation with the peace treaties, there was also the comforting reflection that Ireland had absorbed enough of the government's attention, and that it would do her no harm to realise that she could not hold the limelight all the time.[24] But with the final signing of the Versailles pact it was a constitutional fact that Asquith's 1914 Home Rule Act would automatically come into operation unless something were put in its place. The intriguing question was the kind of Home Rule measure that a Unionist dominated coalition could pass; Lloyd George was determined that it would be a measure indelibly stamped with Unionist approval: there would be no repetition of his 1916 disaster. The government's Irish committee was appointed under the chairmanship of Walter Long, one of the chief instruments of the destruction of the 1916 settlement, but now a Unionist with a difference, in that he was prepared to acknowledge that the absolutism of prewar Unionism was obsolescent. Moreover, Long was willing to meet any forceful nationalist challenge in a 'fair and square fight';[25] which, as the government recruited ex-servicemen to the Royal Irish Constabulary, soon turned out to be neither very square nor fair. Still, Long would assure Irish Unionists, north and south, that there would be no sell-out; and he could perform the same service for the British Unionist Party, for there again his credentials were impeccable.

In October 1919, therefore, Home Rule was taken up yet again by a British government, and came back into British politics for the last time in its Gladstonian form. But the bill that eventually emerged was not traditionally Gladstonian. For the first time the Ulster Question was dealt with, not merely as a matter of exclusion, but in a way that deflected accusations that Britain was determined to maintain a direct and immediate presence in any part of Ireland. The committee considered various options before recommending that there should be two parliaments in Ireland, one for northern Unionists and one for southern Nationalists, with a Council of Ireland to provide both a symbol of, and possibly a bridge to, Irish unity: thus would all Irishmen enjoy self-government; partition would be reconciled with unity, and Britain would place the governing of Ireland at arm's length. The bill was an inspired piece of drafting; and it reflected the changed conditions of British political life, when both major British parties had, in considerable degree, insulated themselves from their erstwhile Irish allies. But the new mood was not only a party political question; Ireland had moved on to the international stage in the war, and she was still a complicating factor in Britain's relations with the world: putting Britain right in the eyes of America and the Dominions was an irresistible argument for Home Rule. The distancing of Liberals and Unionists from the Irish parties, and the refusal of Sinn Fein to take their seats in Westminster, opened the way to the formidable pressure that a united British coalition, backed with armed force, could apply to Ireland: bipartisanship supported by military force was (it was hoped) a means of bringing nationalist Ireland to accept the reality of Home Rule as defined by the British.

The question of Unionist Ulster was not quite the same, for here it was acknowledged by the Irish committee that 'it would be difficult for the government to force through a scheme which was unacceptable both to their friends and to their critics'. The government insisted on the Ulster Unionists accepting a parliament which they did not want, but which was certainly preferable to Dublin rule; but it made a major concession to Unionist Ulster on the question of the area of the new state. The government committee recommended a nine county Northern Ireland, and even the chairmanship of Bonar Law at a crucial stage of the committee's proceedings did not alter this recommendation. But the Ulster Unionists brought all the influence they could muster to bear on the committee. The government felt it had no choice but to concede a six county Northern Ireland and in March 1920 the Government of Ireland bill began its progress towards the statue book, which ended with its becoming law the following December.[26]

As the bill moved inexorably through its parliamentary stages, it was met with a storm of criticism within both Britain and Ireland. But the government knew it could weather the storm. As long as the coalition held, its Irish policy held, and no protests from the now abandoned southern Irish Unionists, Irish Nationalists, nor sections of the British press and political opinion, could shake the government's resolve. The government could rely also on the sheer boredom and fatigue that Irish politics induced in the British public at large, and it could claim, with a reasonable degree of justification, that there was no alternative: a useful political phrase when any alternative seemed to imply a return to the quandaries of the dark days of 1913–14.

The government had, in a sense, made a tacit bargain with the Ulster Unionists: six counties in exchange for the Unionists accepting their half of the double-barrelled Home Rule bill. Nationalists were not yet in the bargaining mood, and here the government must use force to oblige Sinn Fein to accept its share of the bill now on offer. But the government did not have the will to embark on a major coercive campaign in Ireland; instead it resorted to a series of ill-considered and often confused expedients. The violent aspect of the Irish Question now provoked, as it had always provoked, different responses in British politics. 'Black and Tan' recruits to the RIC were intended as a way of fighting a 'police war' in Ireland, instead of the wholehearted onslaught of martial law and army control. But their rough and ready methods, their indiscipline, and their random attacks on civilians as a means of hitting back at ruthless and elusive enemies brought down protest on the government's head from important sections of British public opinion. And however much ministers might defend the government's record in public (and also in private), they were driven by the spring of 1921 to acknowledge that, as Lord Birkenhead put it, the military methods adopted by the government had not kept pace with, or overcome, those adopted by their opponents.[27]

The government maintained informal contacts with various nationalist leaders even when the fighting was at its worst. But it was not until May and June 1921 that Lloyd George turned his full attention to the Irish Question, after months in which there was a hardly a newspaper in Fleet Street that supported his policy: and Lloyd George was a politician who liked to keep in touch with the press. The problem was that coalition politics required a prime minister to consider carefully the mood of his backbenchers; indeed when Lloyd George examined his Irish Committee's Home Rule proposals in November 1919 his first instinct was to test the political mood by placing a series of resolutions before parliament for discussion. If the government were indeed to abandon its parliament for southern Ireland, which opened in 1921 only to close immediately, then Lloyd George must calculate the mood of his supporters, especially in the Tory ranks (Liberals had already expressed their doubts about the direction of government policy). Two events helped him move his policy forward: the recognition that by May 1921 the choice lay between peace talks or an all-out war, and Unionists as much as Liberals were anxious not to commit themselves to this latter alternative without one last attempt at peace; and the intervention of King George V, who, at the opening of the Northern Ireland parliament on 22 June, urged peace and reconciliation – an appeal from the monarch which Unionists would find difficult to set aside.

Lloyd George's pragmatic style was well suited to the Irish Question in this delicate phase in British party politics. He had of course to exercise all his negotiating skills in dealing with representatives of Sinn Fein; but however difficult the task which confronted him in 1921, it was one that could only be seriously jeopardised if the Unionist Party broke ranks and found his terms of settlement unacceptable, as they had in 1916. But Lloyd George never lost touch with his political supporters, or potential opponents, however secretly or deeply he was closeted with Sinn Fein. From the beginning he was careful to associate leading Unionists such as Austen Chamberlain and Lord Birkenhead with his negotiations. His offer of dominion status to the Irish Nationalists was one that met with an enthusiastic response in most Unionist newspapers, and, equally significant, in the Liberal press as well, which declared that the 'English conscience is now clear'[28] and warned of the consequences of a blank refusal on the part of Sinn Fein. No British prime minister, since Pitt the

Younger negotiated the Act of Union, had ever been in such a favourable political position; to say this is not to disparage Lloyd George's great political gifts, but to acknowledge that in 1921, as in 1916, political gifts must mesh with political organisations to produce results. And Lloyd George did produce a result of sorts which, however much it disappointed future hopes that the Irish Question was 'solved', at least restored peace to Ireland and – perhaps its most pressing objective – removed the Irish Question from British party politics.

The only major external problem which threatened the course of the negotiations with Sinn Fein leaders between October and December 1921 was the Ulster Question. Lloyd George's government had created the political entity of Northern Ireland, but it had not so far given it the means, nor the money, through which it could establish itself as a working state. When in 1921 Lloyd George invited the Ulster Unionist government to participate in the negotiations for a settlement, the Northern Ireland Prime Minister, Sir James Craig pondered on the British motivation, and some of his Cabinet wondered 'what was behind the invitation . . . and why should not Ulster be left in peace to set its Parliament in order'.[29] Lloyd George had bargained with Ulster before, in 1916 and (covertly) in 1920 over the Government of Ireland Act. Now he sought once more to take up the Ulster issue, this time as a means of inducing Sinn Fein to accept dominion status and drop their claim for a more ambitious form of self-government, if not actual separation. On 10 November Lloyd George wrote to Sir James Craig proposing that Northern Ireland, while retaining the powers granted to her under the Government of Ireland Act, should exchange her subordination to Westminster for subordination to Dublin, but of course to a Dublin endowed with dominion powers and in the British Empire. Craig appears to have regarded this offer as one that would be difficult to refuse, but he was able to mount a counterattack, using the Unionist Party annual conference to be held in 'Orange Liverpool' as the place and opportunity most likely to embarrass the government. The Unionists were in a dilemma. They could rely on widespread support of pressurising Craig, under the slogan 'Ulster blocks the way'; but they feared a split in the party should Ulster's greatest sympathiser, Bonar Law, return to active politics to save his people from the coalition's Irish policy. However, soundings indicated that while some sympathy with Ulster remained, yet the 'new men who were never engaged in the Irish fights' put the whole loyalty issue in perspective. Moreover, the 'die-hards', as they were soon nicknamed, were threatening the whole negotiations, and their extremism, in endangering what most people in Britain regarded as a 'reasonable' settlement, would have allowed Lloyd George to run a public campaign against Ulster obduracy.

Such an eventuality would have landed not only the Irish Question but the Ulster Question firmly back into the centre of British political controversy, and might have provoked party splits and divisions, with recriminations that would ring down the generations: no-one in the Tory Party ever forgot Sir Robert Peel and 1847. Austen Chamberlain was convinced that his opponents in the Unionist Party could never form a government if the administration fell over its Irish policy; but this would be scant comfort if Unionism were to be irrevocably split. It was easier and indeed more realistic to seek a way round the difficulty; and in the Liverpool conference it was arranged, before the speeches and motions on Ireland were heard and discussed, that there would be no question of the 'coercion of Ulster', but in return the Irish negotiations must be allowed to continue. The die-hards were persuaded to withdraw their resolutions 'except a mild one', and the government's supporters would move an amendment of confidence 'and bless the Irish Conference'.[30] The Tory Party's traditional ability to stage manage its conferences, rather than spill its own blood, stood it in good stead once again; and Lloyd George was left to apply pressure on Sinn Fein, and to seek a way round the partition difficulty with the ambiguous offer of a boundary commission which would adjust the border between Northern Ireland and the rest. The implication was that this would work in favour of reunification, since it would make the Northern Ireland state no longer a viable entity. In any case Michael Collins and Arthur Griffith were by the beginning of December seeking a way out of the Ulster difficulty, for they had made up their minds that the government offer of dominion status, with various negotiated amendments, was an honourable one to accept, and at least offered the chance to develop and foster Irish freedom. Lloyd George was now able to bring the Irish delegates face to face with the stark choice of signing a treaty or precipitating a renewal of the war. They chose to sign.

Realities were breaking in on the Irish Question in the autumn of 1921: Unionist Ulster had realised the dangers of her position, and Craig had, with great persistence, pressed for the transfer of administrative powers such as justice, local government, and public health to be made from the United Kingdom government to the new state to give reality to his rather shaky regime in Northern Ireland.[31] Collins and Griffith had acknowledged the fact that the negotiating game was played out; and the coalition had accepted an Irish settlement that would have been inconceivable even a year earlier. But the reaction in Unionist ranks was mixed. Relief at a settlement, and acceptance of its terms was tempered with a sense that Lloyd George had in some way betrayed the Union: a sense of betrayal sincerely felt by some, but which others expressed knowing in their hearts that it was a betrayal in the best interest of the Unionist Party, and indeed of the future of Unionist, perhaps even British, politics.

IV

The treaty was debated and passed in both houses of parliament on 14 December 1921; and despite Unionist resentment at the surrender to the IRA, as Sir Edward Carson called it, it was safe provided Bonar Law did not emerge as its enemy which, while expressing his misgivings about the conduct of the negotiations, and the pressure exerted by Lloyd George on Unionist Ulster, Law did not care to do. Lord Birkenhead, always a realist in politics, responded to Carson's bitter attack on him for betraying his friends of the prewar stand against Home Rule by declaring that:

it is perfectly true that we have changed our minds more than once in the last three years, and we may change them again. Our difficulties lie in attempting to convince the medievalists among us that the world has really undergone some very considerable modification in the last few years.[32]

But the lingering sense of betrayal was reinforced by the events of the next six months, as Irish Nationalists split over the treaty, and the provisional government seemed anxious to avoid taking a strong line with the anti-treaty groups, and, even, to widen the terms of the treaty in the direction of a more separatist interpretation. This did not lead to a break with Arthur Griffith, Michael Collins and the government of the Irish Free State; Lloyd George knew that no-one in Britain seriously wanted to renew hostilities while the chance of patching up a compromise remained. But it did open the way for the Irish Question to play, for nearly the last time, a major part in British politics.

For the coalition had been declining in popularity with the Unionists in 1921, especially because of the growing fear that Lloyd George was seeking 'fusion' between the parties, a fusion that Unionists feared would eliminate their independence as a party, their identity as a political force. The Irish Question enabled the coalition leaders to re-form, and rally their followers around the manifest need for some kind of Irish settlement to end the 'little war' in Ireland, and bring peace with honour. While the Irish negotiations were at their height, no-one could think of breaking up the coalition. But now that this episode was over, there seemed little reason to regard Lloyd George and his team as indispensable; and the controversy over Ulster in November 1921 had brought Bonar Law out of political retirement to ensure that the government would not, as he feared it intended, 'let Ulster down badly'.[33] Law was, to the Unionist rank and file, an alternative leader and prime minister; and Lloyd George's group of first-class brains was no longer the whole repository of Unionist leadership. Unionists had been promised by Law in 1918 that coalition would not destroy party unity and party identity; now he might be persuaded to prolong his emergence from retirement in order to undermine the coalition that was threatening to undermine his party.

Ireland provided further material for the restive Unionist ranks to complain about: when Austen Chamberlain visited the widow of Sir Henry Wilson, the former CIGS, who was shot dead by Irish gunmen outside his home, he was greeted with the word 'murderer'. Unionists combined resentment at the deteriorating situation in Ireland, which ended with the outbreak of civil war in June 1922, with a general desire to put the coalition to the proof, for it seemed to have outlived its usefulness, defined by its leaders as combining 'all that is reasonably progressive in the Unionist Party with what is sound . . . in the Liberal Party'.[34] Law had earlier expressed his dissatisfaction with the government's Irish policy and his belief that he had been mistaken in supporting the treaty. In October 1922 he was persuaded, with characteristic diffidence, to accept the leadership of anti-coalition discontent; and at the vital meeting called by Unionists to review the coalition he let it be known that he was available to take the party out of the coalition wilderness, reminding it of the splits it had endured in 1846–47. The Unionists voted to withdraw from the coalition; Lloyd George immediately resigned; and Law was formally elected leader on 23 October, becoming prime minister the same day.

Yet even while Unionist discontent with the consequences of the Anglo-Irish Treaty had been gathering strength in the first six months of 1922, the effect of that last great struggle over the Union was having its impact on the role of the Irish Question in British politics. The process by which government policy had been distancing Ireland from Great Britain – in the 1920 Government of Ireland Act, and now in the Anglo-Irish Treaty – was demonstrated in the two great issues which confronted the government in the aftermath of the treaty: law and order (especially sectarian violence in Ulster), and the complexities of southern politics, as the pro-treaty politicians sought their way out of the divisions and dangers of civil war. The British government regarded Collins' and Griffith's efforts to avert an open split as 'feeble' and 'apologetic';[35] it deprecated the provisional government's decision to postpone elections for a new government until June 1922, and then its attempt to exclude the treaty as an election issue by apportioning the seats in the new parliament according to the existing proportions in Dail Eireann. But it was prepared to wait upon events in the hope that the elections would strengthen the new government's chances of implementing the treaty; and this pragmatic approach paid off when the pro-treaty party won 58 seats and the anti-treatyites only 35. It was only then that the British pressed Collins and Griffith to take a strong line with the anti-treaty forces. Direct intervention, though threatened, was acknowledged to be an unprepossessing alternative.

The problem with the south was inevitably associated with the alarming increase of sectarian violence in the north, for here again the government feared that it might be manoeuvred on to its weakest ground, as the Free State complained about the Unionist government's partiality. The Ulster issue must be 'eliminated'; and the British government proposed a judicial inquiry, preferring this to the Free State's suggestion of the assumption of Britain's direct control over the north.[36] Sir James Craig was able to take advantage of Britain's desire to stand aside to negotiate financial assistance for his government throughout 1922. And when in July 1922 Craig passed a bill abolishing proportional representation for local government elections in Northern Ireland as a means of ensuring the maximum Unionist strength, the British government protested, but eventually acquiesced,[37] rather than risk the resignation of the Northern Ireland government, the resumption of direct rule by Westminster and the revival of what Lord Birkenhead called, in one of his rolling phrases, 'the dying forces of extinct controversies'.[38]

V

The political language now being developed to describe, amongst other things, the Irish Question bears some examination; for the notion of Ireland as a threat, a nuisance, an increasingly obsolescent political issue was one that soon caught hold of the British political vocabulary, and has remained unaltered ever since. Yet it is important not to predate its popularity; for between 1886 and 1914, and especially in the years after 1906, Ireland was a central issue in British politics, although not of course an ever-present one, nor one without an irritating quality, especially to

Liberals. Unionists, however restive they might feel about their relationship with Irish Unionists, acknowledged that, as one of their number put it, 'we exist to oppose home rule'.[39]

By 1918 none of the British political parties existed for reasons to do with Ireland. The concluding of the Versailles Peace Treaties made a solution of the Irish Question imperative. Between 1920 and 1921 Ulster Unionists and Irish Nationalists were coerced or manoeuvred into a position where compromise was more acceptable than complete victory. The reason was that a combination of coalition politics, superior strength and a major shift in British public opinion enabled Britain to insist upon a settlement, first in Ulster, then in the rest of Ireland. It was not the best possible arrangement; nor was it a solution of the Irish Question. But it was one that placed Ireland firmly outside the realm of British party politics. And that fact would exert a profound influence on the shape of Anglo-Irish relations in time to come.

3

A QUESTION OF
CONTAINMENT, 1923–49:
BRITAIN, THE TWO IRELANDS
AND THE COMMONWEALTH

I

The Irish settlement of 1921 changed the form, and, in part, the substance of the Irish Question, and more particularly of the Irish Question in British politics. It was now, perhaps, an Irish Question *for*, rather than *in*, British politics. No longer was it a struggle between Irish nationalists and British Unionists over self-government or its denial; no longer was it shaped by an alliance between Irish Nationalists and British Liberals, and between Irish Unionists (north and south) and Unionists in Britain. This termination of old party ties naturally had an impact on new party images, as the Irish flavour of the British political parties quickly waned, and became residual. It was true that the official name of the Conservatives was still the 'Conservative and Unionist Party', and indeed the Primrose League continued to refer to the 'Unionist Party' during the 1920s. Lady Londonderry even lectured on the 'Meaning of Unionism', while acknowledging, however, that the original idea had 'gone beyond recall'.[1] The Irish representation in the House of Commons was by the terms of the Government of Ireland Act reduced to a mere dozen seats and consisted almost entirely of Ulster Unionists. Liberals were no more inclined to cling to their old image than were Unionists, for Liberals after 1922 had other more pressing concerns, such as the challenge of Labour, which sought to unseat the Liberals with the slogan that Labour was the new progressive party. The removal of the centre of responsibility for Irish affairs from London to the capital cities of two new Irish states, Belfast and Dublin, was bound to have an impact on the British perception of the Anglo-Irish relationship: Irish Questions were now at one remove for the first time since 1800, and it was soon perceived to be advantageous to keep them there. The benefits of this were all too soon borne in on the British political parties; its drawbacks were not to be felt for several generations.

The departure of Ireland from the centre of the British political stage was to have a more general influence. Ireland could still provoke an echo in certain areas of Lancashire, where T. P. O'Connor held on to his Liverpool (Scotland division) seat as he had done since 1885; and he was succeeded by another Irish representative in 1929. But his successor took the Labour whip. And insofar as Irish voters were an identifiable bloc in British cities in the nineteenth century, they now ceased to have any identifiable special Irish political direction, and simply fell in behind the Labour Party. Moreover, the advance of Labour had an impact on the Irish Question, or what was left of it. It obliged Conservatives, in particular, to devise ways of containing the new threat, and reconciling it with the British political tradition. This naturally caused them to pay more attention to purely social and economic issues, a trend discernable in the Lloyd George era. Labour for its part, had no Irish past to live down; or to live up to. It had supported Home Rule all round, federalism and decentralisation in a loose and ill-considered manner before 1922; it protested against coalition policy and especially the violence of the Black and Tan war. Its Irish vote encouraged its rather woolly spirit of goodwill towards nationalism and hostility towards Ulster Unionism, as some kind of capitalist hegemony of the north of Ireland. But its central concerns were nearer home, and resolutions in Ireland, never very committed, soon died out from party conferences.

The decline of the politics of Nationalism and Unionism was reflected in the rapid thinning of interest in Scottish and Welsh Home Rule after the Irish settlement. Scotland had reaped some reward (if such it was) from the Irish Home Rule crisis in the form of pressure from some of her Liberal MPs for a Scottish assembly, especially in the exciting days of 1913–14. Wales, too, had come under the Celtic umbrella, with Lloyd George, a characteristic product of Welsh radical Nonconformity, combining nationalist sentiment with an assault on the privileges of the landlord and the Anglican Church, and even contemplating separatism in the 1890s. But now, deprived of the motor of Irish nationalism, Scottish and Welsh national sentiment lost their momentum. Scotland and Wales were, in any case, travelling in directions rather different from Ireland. Scotland still enjoyed its own educational, legal and ecclesiastical arrangements, which rendered Home Rule hardly necessary; Wales had claimed, and largely received, equality with England, and nationalism had been undermined by its own success. The foundation of Plaid Cymru in 1925, and the Scottish National Party in 1934, did not disturb the surface, let alone stir the depths of British political life. Moreover, the Irish experience showed that nationalism could be a costly and even bloody business. And the main British parties had changed as well. Religion had ceased to be a factor in British politics. No longer were the Nonconformist churches the Liberal Party at prayer; no more would the Conservative Party stand as the embodiment of Anglicanism, of Church and squire; and the Labour Party combined its appeal to the underprivileged in the Celtic fringe with a centralist policy and a personality in which any cultural dimension was wholly lacking.

After 1923, then, it was possible to speak of 'British' politics almost without qualification. This new atmosphere – and the subsequent acknowledgement by British politicians that the 'British' were one nation, but perhaps several, economically deeply divided classes – produced new political obsessions in Great Britain, obsessions in which Irish affairs played little part. But if Ireland was still unappeased; if the treaty settlement of 1921 broke down: then, whether they liked it or not, British statesmen must direct their gaze not only towards the dreary steeples of Fermanagh and Tyrone, but also to the tall, professorial figure of nationalist Ireland's conscience: Eamon de Valera.

II

The British tradition of believing that political problems have solutions seemed vindicated in the treaty settlement of 1921 and the establishment of Northern Ireland and the Irish Free State. The only unfinished business lay in the boundary commission which, under the terms of the treaty, must be invoked should Northern Ireland continue to refuse Dublin sovereignty. This commission was to examine the boundary between north and south and if necessary redraw it 'in accordance with the wishes of the inhabitants, so far as may be compatible with economic and geographic conditions'. The ambiguity surrounding this phrase, and the way in which it might be interpreted by the interested parties, could have provoked a major rift in Anglo-Irish relations and in relations between the Free State and Northern Ireland. The Unionist government in Belfast, for its part, refused even to appoint its representative, and Britain was obliged to appoint a commissioner on Northern Ireland's behalf. The Labour government of Ramsay Macdonald had been only too aware of the dangers of reviving Northern Protestant fears of absorption in a united Ireland, and on 11 June 1924 the army had indicated that at least three divisions of troops and a brigade of cavalry and armoured cars and tanks would be necessary to maintain order if there were to be a plebiscite on the border issue. But if any award favoured the north, then it might be necessary to blockade the Free State. When Stanley Baldwin inherited the problem after the fall of the Labour government, he was well aware of the dangers of right-wing sentiment in his party over the issue, and of an Ulster rebellion should the Northern Ireland state appear threatened by the commission's report.[2]

The issue was resolved through a compromise between the British and Irish governments, who perceived the greater danger lay with change, and that safety resided in maintaining the status quo. The question facing the commission was whether it should work in conformity with the spirit of the Anglo-Irish Treaty, which seemed favourable to the claims of the Free State, or accommodate itself to the new factors created by the continuing existence and growing stability of Northern Ireland. Richard

Feetham, a South African judge, who chaired the committee, interpreted his brief as that of maintaining Northern Ireland as 'the same provincial entity', 'capable of maintaining a Parliament and Government', and urged that the onus of proof lay with those who would change the border: in lawyer's terms, Northern Ireland was innocent until found guilty. This meant that the changes proposed were minimal. No Conservative government wanted to reopen the question of Northern Ireland, partly out of a residual loyalty to former allies, but mainly because of the difficulties that the Ulster prime minister, Sir James Craig, could create if the existence of his state were threatened. William Cosgrave's Free State government was in no mood to provoke serious trouble over the border issue. In October 1925 the commissioners reached agreement on their report, an account of which was published in the *Morning Post* some weeks later. This was correct in general, in that it revealed that any transfer of territory would be minimal, and that nationalist areas in Derry City, Newry, south Down and almost all of Tyrone and Fermanagh would remain under Unionist rule. Premature disclosure made it more difficult for the Free State to accept the commission's findings, and as nationalist opinion in the south hardened against it, a breakdown in Anglo-Irish relations seemed imminent. But Baldwin was careful in devising his response to Nationalist indignation: he employed Lord Salisbury and Sir William Joynson-Hicks, his chief critics in his party, in the subsequent negotiations, thus forging a link between the old Unionism and the new Conservatism; L. S. Amery was also included, as a voice rather more sympathetic to the Free State cause. Baldwin offered the Free State the solatium of the cancellation of £155 million in debts that it had inherited in 1921.[3] When this proved acceptable, and the boundary commission's report abandoned, agreement was quickly, even amicably reached, with Craig declaring that he would 'do anything in reason' to protect the position of Northern Ireland Roman Catholics. Craig and Cosgrave commiserated with each other on the iniquities of proportional representation in parliamentary elections[4] (which the former was soon to jettison). The 1925 compromise was met with rejoicing in Unionist Ulster, relief by the Free State government, and pleasure by the British government, and press, which looked forward to a new era in Anglo-Irish relations.

1926 was an important year in the history of the Irish Question and British politics. The boundary commission was now resolved, and once again the British way of finding solutions to problems had prevailed: sensible men had made sensible decisions. In that year also the Conservative government found itself locked in confrontation with trade unions in the general strike, which was declared by some to be a direct challenge to parliamentary government. This was a groundless fear; but the strike completed the process begun by the Anglo-Irish Treaty of 1921, in that it cleared from the public mind the constitutional issues raised by the Irish demand for self-government, issues which had implications for the whole of the United Kingdom. Parliament had survived; there could not be too much wrong with the system after all; and Britain could go on 'muddling on tolerably well' as she always had done. Soon the onset of economic depression turned public attention even further away from politics to economics, or rather, to the politics of economics.

III

The treaty of 1921, and the boundary commission's demise, placed Ireland outside the mainstream of British politics; but it did not place Ireland outside the British Empire and Commonwealth. Nor could it tow Ireland away into the Atlantic, and end her close proximity with Great Britain. Thus while the Free State was now a Dominion, she was not a Dominion like Canada or Australia, except in constitutional form. She was still in the British archipelago; and she was soon to demonstrate that she was still obsessed with the British relationship. Ireland, therefore, could never be entirely 'outside' British politics: the sea forbade the reordering of British and Irish politics on some central axis; but the Atlantic Ocean forbade Britain and Ireland from going their own ways irrespective of each other's political destiny. The attempt to place Ireland in some kind of 'post colonial' context;

or to regard her as some sort of 'European' country, unnaturally attached to Britain, does not describe the complexity and ambiguity of the Anglo-Irish relationship after 1922. For while there was no longer an Irish Question in British party politics, as there had been since 1886, there was an Irish Question for British politics to cope with as best it could in the harsh and forbidding world of the interwar years.

Ireland was now a dominion; and she could rely on the support of other dominions in many circumstances when it came to pressing the claims of dominion status beyond the limits of 1921. Britain could no longer deal with Ireland as an internal problem, and indeed she had found it increasingly difficult to define the Irish Question as an internal problem from 1916 onwards. The British political generation that had been nurtured on the Irish Question – Lloyd George, Bonar Law, Birkenhead, Austen Chamberlain – was passing or had passed from power, and the new generation was less familiar with Irish issues, or had enough experience of the older generation's difficulties to convince them that familiarity was not to be desired. Labour, for its part, had from the beginning proclaimed itself as a 'detached party listening to what is said'.[5] Public opinion was uninterested and inert, and the party managers saw little profit in trying to arouse the electorate over issues which might best be resolved by the political elite: they had, after all, been publicly exposed over Irish Questions in the recent past, and no-one knew what horrible difficulties might lie in the undergrowth still. And there were no votes in the Irish Question any more. It was best to leave it all to the governing and diplomatic minority, and let public opinion alone.

However, this was not how the view looked from the other side of the Irish sea. Cosgrave's amicable settlement in 1925 raised hopes in Britain that all was now well, and would remain so. But in 1932 Cosgrave was replaced by Eamon de Valera and his Fianna Fail government, which sought to redefine, and rewrite, the constitutional relationship between Britain and Ireland in ways that caused not only anger, but bafflement, in London, and raised serious doubts about de Valera's sanity. Moreover, in the troublesome economic world of the 1930s matters of finance and trade were bound to prove contentious, as the Dublin government sought to establish its credentials as a fully sovereign state, and was prepared to employ economic measures to make good this claim: measures which Britain was quick to reciprocate. Finally, as Britain and her Empire recovered from the immense struggle of the Great War, only to cope with the difficulties of defending herself and her Empire in the deteriorating international climate of the interwar years, the strategic role of Ireland in British defence policy assumed greater importance. Irish nationalist opinion was obsessed with Britain; and de Valera's unappeased nationalism was especially vexatious in the light of the amicable tidying up agreement of 1925. As de Valera and the British government became involved in political and economic conflict in the 1930s, the older, more grievous nature of the Irish Question inevitably came to the surface once again.

These issues never attained the public importance that they had in the earlier phase of the Irish Question, at least not in Britain; in Ireland they were followed with the closest interest, north and south of the border, for whereas the British political elite was adept at managing those issues which it thought best to contain and reserve from too much public scrutiny, Irish opinion in Ulster and the south was more democratic; and Irish political leaders were only too painfully aware of this, especially in the north, where political leaders had at times to fulful the role of political followers simply in order to retain their position. As the Irish Free State sought to widen the terms of the dominion connection in 1926–31 – long before the alarming return of de Valera – Baldwin and MacDonald alike were concerned only to manage the predicament, seek the middle way, and ensure that they were not vulnerable to the charge that they were selling out the British Empire, a charge that they feared some parliamentary die-hards might yet lay at their door. And they maintained that, after all, the British Empire rested upon consent: so the Statute of Westminster, drawn up by A. J. Balfour, nationalist Ireland's most perpetually hostile British foe, acknowledged the dominions' equality with the mother country, with allegiance to the common crown their symbolic constitutional bond.

IV

When de Valera began to apply his mind to Balfour's theoretical propositions, Britain was faced with a dilemma. It was hoped that the Irish electorate might, soon enough, come to its senses, and elect once more a 'pro-British' government in the shape of Cumann na nGaedheal. The national government which took office after the collapse of the Labour administration in 1931 was developing competent and satisfactory domestic strategies, and did not wish to allow Ireland to complicate matters as she had done in the past. Yet de Valera was in power, and in power with his openly declared determination to establish what he called a 'completely free Ireland', warning that although Ireland was 'in the Commonwealth' she was not 'of it'. But she was 'of it' enough to exploit her membership in ways that Britain found it difficult to respond to: the spectacle of the mother country seeking to coerce one of her children might easily arouse the sentiment of the other siblings. And it was against Britain's self-concept to play the part of the great power bullying the little one (some will disagree). The dominions secretary, J. H. Thomas, remarked that:

> Our policy has always been that, if the Irish Free State intends to secede, it should do so by an overt act about which there can be no possible doubt and that we ought not to allow ourselves to be open to the charge that we have forced the Free State out of the Commonwealth.[6]

The British government, however, was faced in de Valera with a master at the art of political manoeuvre; and it was never able to flush its opponent out into the open. De Valera began with a refusal to continue payment of land annuities, due to Britain under the land purchase acts of the Home Rule era, a policy at once popular and exhilarating for his supporters, since it combined the rhetoric of ancient wrongs with immediate tangible benefit for the Irish farmer. J. H. Thomas replied that he did not know 'any party in this House that has ever subscribed to the policy that a bargain or treaty between two sides could with impunity be repudiated by one'.[7] Here was a sound platform for a British statesman to stand upon, for was it not in the British way that gentlemen would never renege upon agreements? Lloyd George spoke darkly of the submarine menace of the Great War; Austen Chamberlain harked back to the treaty settlement of 1921.[8] Thomas's own first instinct to fight was replaced after second thoughts by the desire for some means of reconciliation, as witnessed in his parliamentary statements that Britain had 'gone to the limit of compromise', yet still desired a 'peaceful settlement'.[9] But Thomas was a Labour member of a mainly Conservative national government, and his room for manoeuvre was limited by Conservative anger at de Valera's treachery. Since the limit of compromise was reached with de Valera's refusal to agree to Commonwealth arbitration, and the failure of a con-ference in London in July 1932, there was nothing left for it but to use some means of bringing pressure to bear upon this formidable adversary.

The British government decided to impose a twenty per cent duty on some two-thirds of Irish exports to the United Kingdom to recoup its losses on the land annuities; but it also hoped to bring down the de Valera government and open the way for a return to power of Cosgrave's Cumann na nGaedheal Party which, indeed, intimated to London that de Valera's majority in the Dail might crumble. But both sides to the dispute were concerned to manage the affair; and neither took the extreme steps that were, on the face of it, available. De Valera did not go beyond his protectionist programme, for he knew that to do so might provoke the British to use such weapons as they still possessed in their dealings with Ireland: the refusal to allow Britain to be a haven for the Irish immigrant worker; and the deprivation of Irish citizens living in Great Britain of their rights, possibly their enforced repatriation. The British, for their part, were reluctant to respond in this way, for fear of appearing unreasonable and overbearing in their relations with their smaller neighbour. Even Winston Churchill, ever vigilant on the Em-pire's behalf, admitted that Britain was not going to go to war with Ireland.

De Valera's return to power with a majority in a general election in January 1933 – even if that majority was only one, and then after a by-election in 1934, two – was the mandate that he required to press on with his constitutional changes. The British government knew that it had now little hope of seeing a 'friendly' government in Ireland; and so it prepared itself for the onslaught on the treaty settlement of 1921. This came in the form of a series of legislative acts: the abolition of the oath of allegiance to the Crown in 1933, the abolition of the right of appeal to the privy council, the abolition of the right of the governor general to withhold his assent to bills passed by the Dail; and from 1935–37 the making of a new Irish constitution which, as de Valera put it, would be 'absolutely ours'. In November 1936 he was pushed along by the unexpected crisis in British politics, when King Edward VIII's determination to marry Mrs Simpson provided de Valera with the necessity and opportunity to delete from the constitution all mention of the king and of the representative of the crown whether under this title or under the title of governor general. He also proposed to make provisions for the appointment of all diplomatic consular representatives by the authority of the executive council. These bills were prepared and rushed through the Dail in emergency session.[10]

Once again de Valera found the British unable to use their superior power, or even to mobilise Commonwealth opinion against him. The abdication was a sensitive and complex political problem, requiring all Baldwin's dexterity; it also had the unpleasant undertones of a scandal. No British government could take a stand against de Valera's action on this issue. De Valera now put the finishing touches to his new constitution, published on 1 May 1936, approved by the Dail in June, and then approved by referendum in July. This constitution was the embodiment of de Valera's notion of 'external association' of 1921, by which Ireland was an independent sovereign state, associated as a matter of external policy with the other states of the British Commonwealth. It was not in name a republican constitution; but its reference to the 'inalienable, indefeasible, and sovereign right to chose our own form of government' and its naming of the state as 'Eire' satisfied Irish sentiment over self-government and national unity without risking a major crisis with the British government.

The British response to the new Irish constitution revealed the changed nature of the Irish Question for British politics. No-one now worried about the impact of the problem on British parties, nor on British public opinion. The government's Irish Situation Committee, meeting in May 1936, immediately considered the opinion of the dominions. Baldwin was told that if there was a real chance of the Irish Free State leaving the Empire Britain might have 'serious trouble with the other dominions if we could not justify our attitude and policy by showing that we had done everything in reason and had made every practicable concession in order to secure a comprehensive settlement'. In January 1937 it was acknowledged that the dominions were keen on an Irish settlement. They were originally in sympathy with Britain over the land annuities dispute, but as this dragged on and was obviously political, they thought that the sooner it was settled the better for the Commonwealth image.[11] A meeting of the Imperial Conference in London in May 1937 only confirmed this.[12] The new Irish constitution should not therefore, as the Australian High Commissioner put it, be made an issue of, least of all when 'we appear to be on the eve of a development when we are going to get marvellous cooperation in the commonwealth'.[13]

By 1937 the British and Irish governments were ready for a settlement of the long drawn-out economic war, and the constitutional difficulties between Britain and Ireland. For the British government an Anglo-Irish agreement was particularly desirable, not because of the importance of the Irish Question in British politics, but because of its very unimportance in the light of the great events now threatening in Europe. When Neville Chamberlain's Irish Situation Committee met in December 1937 he declared that 'even an agreement which fell short of being completely satisfactory would be better than the insecurity of the present situation'.[14]

An Irish settlement was therefore the first, hardly noticeable, but significant step on the journey that led to appeasement of Germany and the Munich Settlement of 1938. It was taken by Chamberlain who had earlier emerged as one of the most determined advocates of a firm stand against de Valera on the land annuities dispute. Chamberlain's influence was decisive. He wished to demonstrate to the great powers of Europe that Britain was a country prepared to take matters on trust; that she was willing to negotiate, to make concessions and to live with promises rather than immediate tangible benefits in the belief that these would soften the belligerent nature of the Fascist powers. Moreover, this general approach had a certain local appeal when it came to be applied to Anglo-Irish relations: was not the problem of this relationship caused by lack of trust, lack of mutual respect in the past? Britain might bear some responsibility for this predicament; Britain could now take steps to put matters right. Chamberlain went into his Irish negotiations even stronger than Lloyd George had done in 1921: there was no restiveness in the government nor in the Conservative ranks. His mastery of his cabinet was complete. Everyone in Britain wished him well.

When the conference between the British and Irish representatives began on 17 January 1938 there were three main areas of dispute to be cleared up: the economic war; the question of British access to the 'treaty ports', whose use had been guaranteed to Britain under the terms of the 1921 treaty; and, now back on the agenda for the first time since the treaty negotiations, the partition of Ireland. The latter had not been at stake when de Valera opened his long drawn-out dispute with Britain in 1932; but it rankled his Republican heart, and in the 1930s Nationalist opinion in the south began to reawaken to the reality of partition, and the need to 'do something' about it.[15] These were not exclusive issues; on the contrary, they were interrelated: partition could be an end, or a means to an end, as it had been in 1921; it could still be the weak point in the British defence, the battle which political opinion did not want to fight, and which public opinion in general would not support. The economic settlement would have to take Northern Ireland into account, since the north was deeply concerned about any trade or tariff agreement which might affect her economic position with both Britain and southern Ireland. And Northern Ireland was, as ever, watchful of the British and Irish governments when they put their heads together to discuss matters of mutual interest in a conference in which Northern Ireland was not directly represented. Sir James Craig's decision to call a general election on the eve of the talks irritated British ministers, and was a sign of the difficulties that lay ahead.

The Anglo-Irish talks of January to April 1938 were meant to find what was called a 'final settlement' between Britain and Eire; and in the event three separate agreements were signed. The first relinquished British control of the naval bases granted to her under the 1921 treaty; the second ended the economic war and made considerable concessions to Eire; the third was a comprehensive trade agreement, giving most Eire goods free entry into the United Kingdom market, but with a less favourable reciprocal arrangement for British goods. It was not a set of concessions that might be taken as typical of agreements normally concluded between a powerful country and its rather dependent neighbour, at least, not typical of those relations in the Europe of the 1930s, which were characterised by brute force. But then Ireland was not of the Europe of the 1930s, and neither was the United Kingdom.

When a powerful set of British ministers was closeted in conference with de Valera, and determined to reach agreement so that the way might be cleared for Britain to concentrate on a diplomatic resolution of the German question, agreement was indeed more likely than not. But there was one party which had already suffered in the economic war of the 1930s, and which now had to look to itself once again. When the Irish Question was a deeply divisive one in British politics, between 1886 and 1922, Unionist Ulster was of course able to exploit the political crisis to her advantage; but in 1912–14 she was determined to resist Home Rule, whatever British political parties might do. Now, however, the political context was altered. If Britain no longer wanted an Ulster Question, Ulster no longer wanted to provoke a question for Britain. Thus, while the Northern Ireland government watched the 1938 negotiations with some misgivings, it was reluctant to intervene in such a way as to jeopardise their chances of success. The dominions office was hostile to Northern Ireland, comparing its record on religious toleration unfavourably with that of Dublin;[16] but Sir Samuel Hoare, Home Secretary, and W. S. Morrison, Minister of Agriculture, were more sympathetic. The British negotiating team was obliged to use a mixture of pressure and concession when it came to dealing with Ulster's objection to any economic agreement that might damage her trade further. Chamberlain was anxious to avoid raising the partition question once again, even though he regarded a united Ireland as inevitable:[17] he knew that to force an unacceptable agreement on the north might provoke serious trouble, especially if the Northern Ireland government were to resign on the issue and leave Britain once again with the direct responsibility for governing part of Ireland. Moreover, dominion opinion expected a settlement.

Sir James Craig, for his part, did not want to push matters to a crisis. Although a politician of some personal charm and organisational ability, as he had demonstrated in the Ulster crisis of 1912–14, he was not the man to cope with the blandishments and bribes offered him by civil servants and British ministers in 1938. Malcolm MacDonald, the dominions secretary, admitted that Ulster had 'many friends in the House of Commons', but declared that 'even the best friends of Ulster in this country, if they had the Draft Trade Agreement before them would think twice before rejecting it'. Ulster should be offered a bribe, or 'compensation in other directions for the failure to secure preferential treatment from Eire for goods of Northern Ireland origin'.[18] But the treasury, ever hostile to Northern Ireland as a beggar 'who comes to us when bankrupt', was determined that Ulster should neither stand in the way of a settlement, nor do particularly well out of one. The bribe in the end proved to be an improved share for Northern Ireland in British defence contracts, a promise which was met more through military necessity than genuine desire to help the ailing Ulster economy. British ministers in their dealings with Craig sought to induce him to take what they liked to call the 'broad view'; Craig succumbed, even admitting that he would be satisfied with a 'case that was defensible in his Parliament'.[19] All that was left to do was arrange a carefully-timed announcement of the 'concessions' to Northern Ireland on the same day as the Anglo-Irish agreements were signed, and the Ulster Question remained unasked. As Chamberlain put it, any outright opposition from the north could be made to appear unpatriotic in time of danger, when it was imperative to creative an 'impression of solidarity'.[20]

Management proved effective also in the main aspect of these negotiations, the question of the 'treaty ports'. Early on in the negotiations Chamberlain intimated that he would be prepared to return the ports in return for a defence agreement. This concession deprived de Valera of his bargaining power, for he had nothing left to bargain about. He countered with partition: no defence agreement could be signed unless the British government did something about partition, for which Britain had 'a very definite moral responsibility'. Chamberlain countered with a homely analogy: the agreements represented a three-leafed shamrock, and British public opinion would find it hard to accept the trade and finance agreements without seeing better defence terms. De Valera would only offer verbal concessions: he would not object to references being made in the House of Commons to his speeches in the Dail, speeches in which he would argue that the Irish government would be the sole judge of whether or not Ireland would go to war, and that defence plans would be drawn up on two alternative hypotheses: that Ireland went to war alone, and that British interest would be involved, in which eventually the Irish would 'be glad of (United Kingdom) assistance'. This delphic pronouncement was not acceptable to all the British negotiators; but Chamberlain knew that it represented the best concession he could hope for on defence – a concession that helped persuade him that an unconditional return of the treaty ports was indeed the only option. From now on he referred to the necessity of putting de Valera on his honour: 'he would be not only as good but better than his word'; instead of 'black and white' agreements there would be 'atmosphere' and 'attitude'.[21] With the Ulster difficulty over trade settled by 13 April the way was clear for the defence agreement which handed over the facilities in the ports of Berehaven, Queenstown (Cobh) and Lough Swilly to the Irish government which, de Valera claimed, was a final recognition and establishment of Irish sovereignty in the 26 counties and the territorial seas.

Both Chamberlain and MacDonald were apprehensive about reaction to the agreements. Chamberlain feared that he would be 'accused of having weakly given way when Eire was in the hollow of my hand'. But he consoled himself with the reflection that such methods as he had employed were those that would bring peace to Europe: even the most acrimonious disputes were capable of peaceful resolution, provided that there was 'a spirit of accommodation and goodwill on both sides'.[22] The agreement with Ireland, he was sure, would have repercussions in Berlin. The debate on the agreements in the House of Commons on 5 May 1938 illustrated the mood in Britain and indeed in the dominions. Chamberlain's speech emphasised the fact that a 'general settlement' with Eire justified the making of generous concessions, whereas a 'more limited' settlement would not have done so. A limited agreement would have had to stand 'on its own merits', but the Anglo-Irish agreements stood on something other than their merits. But what were these ulterior merits? L. S. Amery – destined to be the man who helped bring Chamberlain down over appeasement in 1940 – provided the answer:

> I believe that today . . . we are still right in acting as a great nation towards a small one, whom we at any rate regard as a partner in the British Commonwealth of Nations, and whom we still hope to see in the fullest sense some day a partner, acting with the very maximum of forebearance and generosity.

Partnership would generate partnership; generosity would bring forth generosity.

Chamberlain and MacDonald, understandably enough, overstated the benefits of the agreements to Britain, and continued in their spirit of wishful thinking that had characterised their whole negotiating strategy. To be fair, there was little benefit in retaining the control of the ports in wartime against the will of the Irish government and electorate; but if Chamberlain hoped that he would prepare the way for Irish support in the event of war, he was much mistaken: no Irish prime minister could have taken his country into war on the side of Britain after the catastrophes of 1916–18. Winston Churchill claimed that the government 'seemed to have given everything away', with nothing gained in return. De Valera had repudiated the 1921 treaty; why did ministers think they could trust him now? The treaty ports were the 'sentinel towers of the western approaches', and the primary purpose in holding them was the defence of Britain.

What would happen if Ireland declared her neutrality? Then de Valera might demand the surrender of Ulster as an alternative to declaring neutrality.[23]

But Churchill was an isolated figure in British politics, discredited by his vociferous opposition to any steps towards Indian self-government in the 1930s. Churchill's impotence contrasted with Chamberlain's strength. Stanley Baldwin bequeathed him an organised, popular and disciplined Conservative Party that was the most powerful force in British politics, dominating the national government in 1937 and contrasting with the weakness of the opposition. Chamberlain for his part was a formidable and prestigious successor to Baldwin, and a leader who could make the party feel the weight of his authority. Chamberlain hoped that appeasement would win Irish Nationalist goodwill; but de Valera looked back on the 1938 agreements as his finest hour because this was a guarantee of Irish neutrality, not because they opened a new chapter in Anglo-Irish relations: rather, the agreements opened an old one that he feared had been closed in the hated treaty of 1921, in that they were a visible and real affirmation of Irish sovereignty. Some nationalists hoped that de Valera's victory over Chamberlain might be repeated on the issue of partition. De Valera informed the Dail that he had tried to persuade London of the importance of the partition question; and he presented the British with a list of Nationalist grievances in the North.[24]

Malcolm MacDonald had promised himself to 'go quietly and carefully' into the matter; and Sir Henry Batterbee, assistant under-secretary at the dominions office, read the evidence on Unionist discrimination against the Roman Catholic minority and concluded that

> the bias of the Northern Ireland authorities is bound to be in favour of those who are supporters of the present regime: it is everywhere inimicable to good and impartial administration where Government and Party are as closely united as in Northern Ireland.

This was a fair and judicious verdict on the Northern Ireland Problem. But the Home Office, faced with the consequences of this predicament, lifted the lid, only to replace it quickly. Like

the British government, its own self-image and political require-
ments caused it to fly in the face of the evidence. To do
otherwise, to break official silence on Northern Ireland, would be
to admit that the Home Office had done less than its duty by the
Northern Ireland Catholic since 1921. When Joynson-Hicks
wrote to Craig to tell him of a deputation from the Northern
Ireland Labour Party which was protesting about the abolition of
proportional representation for Stormont elections in 1929, he
suggested that Craig might care to discuss the matter, adding
however, that 'I "know my place", and don't propose to interfere'.[25]

This (perfectly natural) desire to see Ireland as it should be,
rather than as it was, and to ignore the darker aspects of the Irish
political perception, north and south, was characteristic of the
British desire to prevent the return of the Irish Question in any
serious form after 1926. It was not without significance that the
management of the Irish Question fell to the Conservative Party,
now shorn of its early ideological commitment to the Union and
the Unionists of Ireland, and set firmly on its modern pragmatic
course – or perhaps restored to that course after the heady, but
dangerous, days of 1912. But not even the Conservative Party,
powerful in parliament and the country, and powerfully led by
Neville Chamberlain, could dam the waters of politics in Ireland.
Hardly was the ink dry on the Anglo-Irish agreements than de
Valera launched an anti-partition campaign organised by his
Irish Anti-Partition League. Tension between north and south
increased after the arrest under the Northern Ireland Special
Powers Act of Eamonn Donnolly, an Ulster Nationalist, for
agitation against partition. And when de Valera refused to allow
a British warship to take part in a regatta in Cobh, Edward
Stanley, MacDonald's successor at the dominions office, com-
plained that such action was not the way to 'woo the North'.[26]
De Valera's support of British policy over the Munich crisis in
September 1938 did not fulfil the British expectation that he
would turn verbal backing into concrete assurances over the use
of the treaty ports. And Northern Ireland Unionists were unlikely
to take comfort from de Valera's comparison between the Ulster
Catholic minority and the Sudeten Germans, and his comment

that 'there was a time that if he had felt strong enough he would have moved his troops up to the line to which he thought he was justly entitled, just as Hitler was doing'.[27]

Even the dominions office began to feel impatient with de Valera's failure to 'woo' the north; and it was with perfect justification that MacDonald minuted that 'the two barriers to a united Ireland at the moment are Eire and Northern Ireland: the United Kingdom is no bar'. This does not explain the failure of the Home Office to follow up the lesser – but in a sense far more important – issue of the relationship between State and citizen in Northern Ireland itself. But it would be unrealistic to seek to lay a burden of guilt at Britain's door. For Britain was torn between the realisation that all was not well in the north – a realisation that occurred and reoccured in 1923, and 1938 – and the desire to avoid opening up an issue that could bring nothing but trouble to the British government, perhaps even landing it with the unenviable task of resuming the government of Northern Ireland. Pragmatism and discretion might meet their match in the likes of Portadown and Dungannon.

V

It might not, in the event, triumph even in Dublin, where de Valera's own pragmatism and dominance matched that of Chamberlain in London, but where it was tempered with an awareness of the danger of Fianna Fail's outflanking by more extreme Republican forces. When de Valera sought to reopen the partition question with Chamberlain, he was advised that the British could do nothing without a change in public opinion in Britain, and he advised de Valera to evangelise the British public on the issue.[28] This was a shrewd method of deflecting de Valera from the centre of power in London to the outer – and somewhat nebulous – reaches of public opinion. While the anti-partition campaign in Britain was under preparation, the IRA issued its own ultimatum to the British foreign secretary and began a bombing campaign in British cities. De Valera's difficulties were increased by the outbreak of war in September 1939, a war which Northern Ireland joined, rather ostentatiously, but in which de Valera's Ireland remained neutral. Any advantages that de Valera had gained in his dealings with British politicians in 1938 were quickly lost, especially when the one important British critic of the Anglo-Irish agreements, Winston Churchill, returned to the Admiralty, from where he was quick to describe the Irish position over the 'treaty ports' as 'profoundly unsatisfactory' from the naval point of view.[29]

However, the British unwillingness to bully her small neighbour caused Churchill to stay his hand. After the fall of France in May 1940 the British government offered de Valera the choice of accepting the principle of Irish unity in return for immediate Irish entry into the war: the interests of Northern Ireland, he declared, should not be allowed to stand against the vital interests of the British Empire; and he asked Craig 'what conciliatory gesture under the circumstances the people of Northern Ireland would be prepared to make'. Chamberlain's overture shocked the Northern Ireland government, with Craig declaring that he was 'disgusted' by 'such treachery to loyal Ulster': 'we are closing the gates as our ancestors did at Derry'.[30] In the event de Valera preferred neutrality to some – probably undeliverable – promise that Britain should do her best to persuade Northern Ireland to end partition; and he had his doubts about Britain's ability to win the war anyway. British romantic feeling over the old friend – the Ireland that had after all been part of the United Kingdom for over 100 years – had its last fling when the United States of America entered the war in December 1941. Churchill, now prime minister, appealed to de Valera that 'Now is your chance. Now or Never. A Nation once again'. De Valera took this to mean that the British were once again contemplating a move on partition in return for Irish involvement on the allied side, but he was informed that what Churchill meant was that by entering the conflict 'Ireland would regain her soul'.[31]

The war saw a decisive shift in the British perception of the Irish Question. With Irish neutrality affirmed, and Northern Ireland's participation not only a reality, but a real necessity to the British war effort, above all with the departure of Neville

Chamberlain from British politics, Britain came to view Dublin's political ambitions with a less favourable eye. Relations between Northern Ireland and Eire were strained throughout the war years; but they were now set in a changing context, and even the United States lost sympathy with nationalist anti-partition feeling because of Eire's refusal to participate in the war, while noting also that there was among British cabinet ministers 'a definite weariness if not disgust with the subject of Ireland'.[32] This disgust was increased when, on the death of Hitler, the Irish government conveyed its sympathies to the German ambassador. Churchill took the opportunity to rebuke de Valera for 'frolicking' with the German and later with the Japanese representatives to his heart's content, a phrase which he later regretted using, but which undoubtedly conveyed the British sense of frustration at Eire's role in the great crisis of Europe. Moreover, Irish neutrality and British involvement opened up a great emotional and political gap between Britain and Eire. It was true that many southern Irishmen served in the British armed forces; but Eire was one of the very few European countries not touched by the great struggle; and Irish neutrality, not only in the war but after it, seemed to Britain an expensive luxury in a world divided by the great ideologies of democracy and communism.

This placed Unionist Ulster in an unusually favourable position with all sections of British opinion, and even with what it always tended to regard as its most potentially dangerous foe, the British Labour Party. It was true that the Labour Party had within its backbenchers the suspiciously named 'Friends of Ireland' group, which even went so far as to support the young Desmond Donnelly as Labour candidate for the Northern Ireland Westminster constituency of Down. Donnelly's campaign, in June 1946, provided some interesting diversions for the local press, British reporters covering the election, and possibly even the electorate, which was informed that the election issue was 'socialism versus capitalism', and that the decision of a Labour MP to stand in an Ulster constituency was a sign of 'more realism in politics, an end to the nationality and religious feuds which for so long had kept Eamon de Valera in power in Dublin and Sir Basil Brooke unchallenged in Belfast'. The Labour government, he assured people, was not seeking to undermine the constitutional position of Northern Ireland, and one of the Friends of Ireland group assured the electorate that his organisation did not stand for uniting Ulster and Eire. Donnelly polled a respectable 28,846 votes, coming second in the poll to the official Unionist, and ahead of an unofficial and a democratic Unionist: but he certainly gained the Nationalist vote, for no Roman Catholic candidate stood in the election. His campaign failed to convince the author of a letter signed 'No popery my Dear' which urged him to 'tell the people it is popery you are fighting for instead of Labour, what are the friends of Ireland financed for a Popish state' (sic).[33]

In his campaign Donnelly permitted himself one direct word of warning to the voters: to return a Unionist, he alleged, would be interpreted by the Labour government as giving 'sanction to the violent criticisms which are being made on them on this side of the channel'. Sir Basil Brooke, Prime Minister of Northern Ireland, confided that he was concerned lest it might be 'part of Labour policy to try to create conditions whereby we may be forced into the Free State', and hoped to use Northern Ireland's strategic position to establish her case for staying as she was. And the Dominions and Home Office showed an unusual degree of interest in the position of the Roman Catholic minority. It is clear that there was friction between the two governments in the early years of the Labour administration, especially over Northern Ireland's decision not to introduce 'one man, one vote' in local elections.[34] But this did not reflect the British cabinet's general attitude to Northern Ireland, which was revealed in a memorandum by Herbert Morrison submitted to the cabinet in September 1946, which declared that Sir Basil Brooke was 'most reasonable and cooperative . . . the Unionist Party is by no means wholly a Conservative Party'. Morrison urged his colleagues 'not to hurry the partition issue'. Time would heal this as it healed all things; and in any case British opinion was very conscious of Ulster's participation in and loyalty during the war, while Eire remained neutral.[35]

VI

The Northern Ireland and Labour governments found no difficulty in working together, despite some backbench Labour unrest about the nature of the Unionist regime; and it was against this background of British disillusionment with Eire, and gratitude to Northern Ireland, that the Unionist government was able to obtain a guarantee of its constitutional position within the United Kingdom that was denied it in 1939. The IRA's campaign in Britain in January 1939 seemed to offer the Unionists an advantage with British political opinion that they sought to exploit, but their appeals for a British public affirmation of Northern Ireland's right to stay in the United Kingdom, and for a promise of British assistance should the need arise, were turned down. Lord Londonderry believed that the British 'can always put on a squeeze ... without appearing to coerce, and a Socialist Government would certainly do this'.[36] But in 1949 a Socialist government, far from squeezing the North, agreed that 'no change should be made in the constitutional status of Northern Ireland without Northern Ireland's free agreement'.

This assurance was not the result of a deliberate or premeditated policy by the British, which hoped not to be drawn on the matter of partition. On the contrary, it arose out of the Eire government's decision to leave the Commonwealth, and sever the last remaining links left by de Valera's 1937 constitution. This was the work of de Valera's political opponents, a coalition of Fine Gael, Labour and other opposition parties including the deeply Republican Clann na Poblachta Party led by Sean MacBride. The repeal of the 1936 External Relations Act, which had given the British crown the (rather tenuous) 'authority ... to act in international affairs on behalf of this country' was announced by the Taoiseach, John A. Costello, in September 1948. Attlee's government was a firm upholder of the Commonwealth and Empire: the decision to 'quit India' was not the beginning of a general retreat from Empire. But it was faced with the same dilemma that inhibited all British governments, that if they were to adopt too strong a line, and treat Eire as a wholly foreign power, then the practical difficulties would be greater for the United Kingdom than they would be for Ireland; and Britain would lose the sympathy of the other dominions always assiduous protectors of their newest member. Attlee was unable to make good his earlier threats that there might be serious consequences, particularly over Irish nationality and trade preferences. British political culture, and the political culture of the Commonwealth, once again shaped the British response to the Irish Question, and in ways that modified what might be regarded as the natural response of a large country to its small neighbour.

But British anger at the preremptory nature of the Irish departure from the Commonwealth, and concern for Northern Ireland's strategic importance, enabled the Ulster Unionists to press home their advantage at last. This was not all or even mainly because of Sir Basil Brooke's persuasive style. Rather, it reflected broader British interests which happened to coincide with those of Northern Ireland. It was, wrote the Cabinet secretary Norman Brooke:

> a matter of first class strategic importance for this country that the north should continue to form part of His Majesty's dominions. So far as can be foreseen it will never be to Great Britain's advantage that Northern Ireland should form part of a territory outside H. M.'s jurisdiction. Indeed it seems unlikely that Great Britain would ever be able to agree to this even if the people of Northern Ireland desired it.[37]

Following a visit by Sir Basil Brooke to Chequers in November, 1948 Attlee announced to his cabinet that he had given Brooke 'on behalf of the United Kingdom government, an assurance that the constitutional position of Northern Ireland would be safeguarded', adding 'in a reply to a further question, that he was at liberty to say publicly that he had received that assurance'. The Ireland Act, of June 1949, declared that:

> It is hereby declared that Northern Ireland remains part of His Majesty's dominions and of the United Kingdom and it is hereby affirmed that in no event will Northern Ireland or any part thereof cease to be part of His Majesty's dominions and of the United Kingdom without the consent of the parliament of Northern Ireland.

This not only recognised existing facts; it also represented a real advance for the Ulster Unionists, including the insertion of a guarantee that 'any part' of Northern Ireland (including Nationalist areas) could not have its legitimacy called into question: a final burial for the Boundary Commission of the 1921 Anglo-Irish Treaty.

Attlee was anxious to stress that it was not the British, but the Irish government that had, in Costello's words 'tightened the ligature fastened around the body of Ireland'.[38] The state of Northern Ireland, which had its shaky origins in 1920, which looked in 1921 and 1922 as if it could not survive, which might have been compromised by the boundary commission in 1925 had, within another 25 years, achieved a guarantee of the sanctity of partition, embodied in a law passed by the Westminster parliament, though Attlee had on several occasions warned Ulster Unionist ministers that no parliament could bind its successor, and that a subsequent parliament could 'repeal or revoke' such a declaration.[39] And while it was true that the debate on the Ireland Act aroused opposition and protest in Labour ranks, it provoked only 23 MPs, including tellers, to support an amendment to delete the clause relating to partition.

The Ireland Act could be regarded as that 'final settlement' of the Irish Question sought by Gladstone, Asquith, Lloyd George and Neville Chamberlain. For it was linked with a refusal by the British to treat Irish citizens living in Britain as 'foreigners', or to deprive them of a vote in British elections, or of their rights under the British welfare state. It is only fair to say that any other policy would have caused as many difficulties for Great Britain as for Ireland. Still, with Northern Ireland satisfied, and the south now secure in its Republican destiny, it might appear that indeed the Irish Question was no longer an issue for the British political elite, just as it had long since ceased to be one for the British public at large. Such hopes were momentarily disturbed by the vigorous anti-partition campaign launched by all southern political parties in the wake of the Ireland Act, in which the act was denounced as 'hostile . . . towards the Irish people', with de Valera warning ominously that 'if they tried to put new bars to the door we are going to add new pieces to the might of the battering ram'. But all this propaganda, like so much political propaganda, began and ended at home. It had no impact on the north, except to raise further the political temperature there by its rancour, as futile as it was vigorous. Moreover, the whole experience effectively ended such anti-partition feeling as still existed in Britain after 1921. When Sean MacBride spoke at the Royal Institute of International Affairs to argue the case against partition, he stressed that his claims were 'reasonable, logical and democratic'. But in the discussion afterwards it became clear that his audience, though not unsympathetic, entertained doubts about his logic, and thought that he had best take up his case with Belfast rather than London.[40]

After 1949 the Irish Question went out of fashion even in the closed, elite world of British politics, just as it had for the 'democracy'. Ireland was not even a significant factor in British Commonwealth and foreign affairs as she had been in the interwar years, and especially between 1937 and 1940. Anthony Eden expressed the hope that the new republic would 'play a part in the regional arrangements now being formed to buttress peace',[41] but Ireland's refusal to join the Atlantic Alliance put her outside the mainstream not only of British but of west European politics. So easily did Ireland slip out of British politics after 1949 that no-one in Britain really noticed it; and few in the post-1950 political generation could even recall that there had been an Irish Question in British politics, let alone believe that it had occupied so much time and effort in British political generations since 1868. Herbert Morrison summed up the prevailing climate of opinion when he declared at the 1949 Labour Party conference that 'we do not want to interfere with the internal politics of Ireland and, with great respect, we would like Ireland not to interfere with the internal politics of the United Kingdom'.[42] This of course ignored the fact that Northern Ireland was, in a sense, part of the 'internal' politics of the United Kingdom. But political amnesia set in. When British politicians and public were once again brought face to face with the Ulster crisis in the 1960s, they had no political memory to assist them to come to grips with, let alone develop insight into, that most complex and vexatious of problems: Northern Ireland. They had only the instinctive belief that, in the British tradition, problems were capable of resolution. It was not one that was to help them in this most recent and intractable phase of the Irish Question.

4

A QUESTION OF BIPARTISANSHIP, 1950–86: BRITISH POLITICS AND THE NORTHERN IRELAND PROBLEM

I

When the Labour government passed the Ireland Act in 1949 it seemed that the Irish Question had passed out of British politics, if not out of British history. But it could be argued that the general and more famous, social legislation of that government was ultimately of greater significance for the future of Northern Ireland at least, and therefore of the whole of Ireland and indeed of the United Kingdom. The Labour government's implementation of the welfare state and the national health service, which built upon the wartime Beveridge report on the social services, was intended to bring about at least a modicum of comparability between the social and economic development of the various regions that comprised the kingdom. And while individual members of the Unionist Party might entertain suspicions about the nature of 'socialism', they could hardly stand idly by and see policies introduced in the English regions, Scotland and Wales which affected those industrially disadvantaged areas, which could with considerable benefit be extended to Northern Ireland. As J. M. Andrews, Northern Ireland's prime minister who succeeded Sir James Craig in 1940 put it:

> What keeps the matter right in Great Britain is the fact that there are great rich areas such as London which help to carry the burden of the areas not so favourably circumstanced. Our claim here is that as part of the U.K. we have the right to expect the same security.[1]

This claim was fully met by the Attlee government. And the entry of Northern Ireland into the welfarism of the United Kingdom had important consequences for her people. It further widened the gap between Northern Ireland and Eire, and it gave Northern Ireland a greater tangible benefit from the Union than ever before. No-one could ignore the implications of the welfare state for Catholic and Protestant alike. Some Unionists entertained doubts about the beneficial effects of social security and especially family allowances on the larger Roman Catholic family. But they knew better than to let this prejudice stand in the way of the principles enunciated by Andrews in 1943. And while it was some years before the new politics had their full effect, the rising standards of living, and, more important, the rising standard of expectations of her people must exercise considerable influence on the Northern Ireland state.

This influence was slow to make itself felt. The old border/nationalist/IRA combination was given a new airing with the 152,000 votes collected by Sinn Fein abstentionist candidates in the Westminster general election of 1955, a result at least partly attributable to the political frustration experienced by the Roman Catholic minority and the ineffectiveness of its political representatives in Stormont. This vote was taken by militant Republicans as a sign that the minority wished to see a renewal of the armed struggle to abolish the border. An IRA campaign was launched in 1956 with a series of explosions in remote customs posts; it caused much damage and some loss of life, and worsened relations between north and south, where signs of ambiguity – the 'each way bet' – on the use of violence to achieve unification aroused Unionist anger. But the campaign lost its way in the face of Roman Catholic apathy or outright rejection in the north; and when the IRA called off its campaign in February 1962 it complained bitterly (and accurately) that 'foremost among the factors responsible for the ending of the campaign' was the attitude of the 'general public whose minds have been deliberately distracted from the supreme issue facing the Irish people – the unity and freedom of Ireland'.[2]

If this was indeed the 'main issue' for the 'Irish people', it was not one shared by the British government and public opinion.

The IRA campaign of 1956–62 passed almost unnoticed in the British press and parliament, with only the occasional Sunday newspaper offering somewhat sensational accounts of forays on the border. British troops were employed in the anti-IRA campaign, but only as a secondary supporting force, with the Royal Ulster Constabulary and the Special Constabulary assuming the main responsibility for operations. The Northern Ireland government pressed Sir Anthony Eden for some supportive statements; and, although his government was suffering from the aftermath of the Suez adventure, Eden did speak up with a Commons statement on 19 December. But the Dublin government led by John A. Costello was hardly less firm in its opposition to the IRA, and it was replaced by the even more firm government of de Valera, returned to power yet again in the general election of March 1957 after a campaign in which the Irish political parties vied with each other in stressing a law and order policy – a policy which de Valera carried out when he interned IRA suspects. Anglo-Irish relations easily survived the IRA campaign, and both Britain and Ireland moved into the 1960s in a mood that has been described as 'the end of ideology', when politics would be replaced by the management of resources, and political parties would compete against each other, not on the basis of ideas, and the clash of ideas, but on who could manage best.

Even in Northern Ireland, where political tension was never very far away on the great set-piece occasions like 12 July, this new, modernising mood seemed to have effect; but, as it turned out, one that occasioned a new and lasting crisis, and took Northern Ireland and the Irish Question back into the British political limelight. This hardly seemed possible in the early 1960s, when a new Northern Ireland prime minister, Terence O'Neill, replaced Lord Brookeborough and offered not only Northern Ireland but the British government and public a new, up-to-date image of Ulster Unionism, in tune with the optimistic, non-ideological era. O'Neill's policies, or at least his intentions, consisted of an attack on Northern Ireland's chronic economic weaknesses as well as some moves towards modifying her sectarian image. Plans to attract new investment were parallelled by visits to Roman Catholic schools, talks with leaders of Catholic opinion and overtures generally to the minority. But this new look Unionism would have to struggle against both Roman Catholic impatience at the slow pace of reform, and Unionist doubts about the whole strange and perilous episode. For 're-forms' in the Northern Ireland context must disturb local Unionist hegemony in such areas as local government franchise, local political boundaries and local authority responsibilities, where the allocation of housing was a particularly vexatious issue. By the mid 1960s Northern Ireland was still a peculiar political culture, with the 'new spirit' in politics, rising living standards, and yet a sense of unease among Protestant groups that reform was going too fast, and among Roman Catholic groups that it was not going nearly fast enough. Even the developing prosperity had its sectarian implications, as the welfare state, and a growing willingness of Roman Catholics to stay in Northern Ireland rather than emigrate in larger number than Protestants, inevitably revived the question of political arithmetic; some Unionist opponents of O'Neillism, led by the Reverend Ian Paisley, drew attention to the dire implications for Protestantism should the Roman Catholic population continue to rise, numerically as well as politically.

All this went mainly unnoticed in Great Britain, until the media began to pay increasing attention to the rising political tensions in the north, especially after the murder of a young Catholic barman in June 1966, and the growing expectation that annual parades in the summer marching season might end in violence. But relations between London and Dublin had never been better, especially when in 1965 Great Britain and the Republic inaugurated a major trading partnership that seemed to lock them in a mutually self-interested relationship. And when leaders of the minority in the north began to look, not to Dublin, but to London, for political assistance in bringing pressure on the Unionist government to increase the pace of reform, they soon gained a sympathetic hearing, especially from Labour backbenchers, elected in 1964 in a mood of modernising reformism: if this was an Irish Question, then it was an Irish Question with a difference, and one that could, apparently, be accommodated easily within the British political system.

Labour interest in Northern Ireland came initially from the activities of a few MPs with Irish connections, either in their constituencies, or through their contacts with members of the Northern Ireland minority. Paul Rose owed his involvement to a talk on civil liberties to 'an Irish group in Manchester in 1962'; when asked about Northern Ireland in the 1964 general election he gave a 'solemn undertaking' to visit it, and a year later he founded the 'Campaign for Democracy in Ulster', largely inspired by the Dungannon-based campaign for social justice. But the first veil of ignorance that had to be lifted was that of his own party, which, as he put it, 'knew more about Saigon or Salisbury' than about Stormont. Yet it cannot be said that Rose was himself wholly consistent in his belief that Northern Ireland must conform to British ideas of citizenship; for he described any proposal to increase the number of Northern Ireland seats at Westminster as implying the 'complete integration of Northern Ireland into the United Kingdom', and therefore a proposal of 'acute insensitivity'.[3] This double standard – that Northern Ireland must be integrated in one sense, but still kept at arm's length in another – was to bedevil Labour, and indeed British, perception of the new Irish Question that was emerging in the 1960s. But for the moment those MPs who had an interest in the minority predicament were able to avoid the implications of their own contradictory position. Visits were made to the north by three Labour MPs in 1967 at the invitation of Gerry Fitt, a Republican Labour MP elected to Westminster for West Belfast in March 1966. Meanwhile the campaign for social justice in Northern Ireland became affiliated to the National Council for Civil Liberties in 1965. British criticism of the Northern Ireland government began to mount, with the phrase 'Britain's political slum' coined by the media; and the Campaign for Democracy in Ulster called for a royal commission to investigate the working of the Government of Ireland Act of 1920.

The Labour government, however, was somewhat behind its backbench group in evolving a policy for Northern Ireland. The prime minister, Harold Wilson, encouraged Westminster to take an interest in Irish matters, ending the long established convention that matters peculiar to Northern Ireland were outside the legitimate area of debate for the House of Commons. When Wilson and his Home Secretary, Roy Jenkins, met Terence O'Neill in August 1966 he drew attention to the fact that O'Neill's government was obtaining financial assistance from the British Treasury, and that it was difficult to justify this to MPs and some members of the cabinet without a more liberal regime in Ulster. At the same time he praised O'Neill's 'courage and resolve', and, acknowledging that O'Neill had made more progress in tackling discrimination than all his Stormont predecessors, decided 'to press him no further for the next few months'.[4]

From 1967, however, it was increasingly difficult for the British government to depend upon O'Neillism as a reforming force and one, moreover, that would stand between the government and some more radical intervention in Ulster politics. The founding of the Northern Ireland Civil Rights Association was a sign that minority politics were moving into a more direct and possibly even militant phase. It was also a movement whose style and method could not but attract media attention, not only in Great Britain but throughout the world, with its marches, calls for human rights and use of the language so effectively employed by Black civil rights leaders in the United States of America. The NICRA tacitly, and in some cases openly, recognised the constitutional position of Northern Ireland, since its call was for British standards of social justice to be applied there; but its challenging style was perceived by many Unionists, and especially the Protestant working classes, as a threat both to Protestant social position, and to the stability of the state itself. Demonstrations were met by counter demonstrations, marches by counter marches. It is in retrospect easy to blame the Labour government for not foreseeing the growing seriousness of the crisis; but in August 1968 Terence O'Neill hardly noticed a civil rights meeting in Dungannon, where Catholic complaints against Unionist discriminatory policies were especially bitter, reflecting that 'Northern Ireland being a country of marches, one tended to accept these things as normal'. O'Neill, on holiday in England, scanned his *Times* for news of the incident which, his permanent secretary informed him by telephone, has occasioned 'some anxious moments'; but his paper was full of stories of the Russian invasion of Czechoslovakia.[5]

The Dungannon march failed to hit the headlines; and it must be remembered that Ireland was, for British politics, always an 'issue', that is, one that must be noticed, and must catch the British imagination, before it could be acknowledged or even defined. So far it had received sporadic attention from the media, and some professional interest from only a few MPs. But the Derry civil rights march of October 1968 dramatically changed the picture. Not only did three Labour backbenchers attend the march and witness the rough and summary dispersal of the civil rights supporters by the RUC; television was on the spot and showed to a British audience not only the unacceptable face of Stormont, but a political predicament whose existence had hitherto been scarcely known. The NICRA included people of known Republican sympathies and indeed former members of the IRA; but its propaganda campaign, aided by the brutal and ill-judged Unionist response (both official and, on the streets, unofficial) was inspired. A list of reasonable reforms, such as an end to discrimination in housing, the ending of the Special Powers Act, the disbanding of the Ulster Special Constabulary, were not directly 'nationalist' aims; and the call for a 'one man one vote', which referred to local elections, was regarded by many in Britain as referring to Stormont (and possibly Westminster) elections as well. Few in the NICRA decided that it was worthwhile to disabuse British public opinion of this misapprehension.

British politicians and the British media took the first steps into the Northern Ireland crisis in the conviction that they were rectifying defects in a part of the United Kingdom where British standards of democracy and the British idea of civil society had not so far prevailed. A civil society, it was believed, could be created by pressing a beleaguered Unionist government, now under increasing attack from Unionists outside, and filled with doubt within about the efficacy of O'Neillism, to force the pace of reform. On 5 November Wilson interviewed O'Neill and stressed Labour's 'determination' about reforms and the establishment of 'human rights' in Northern Ireland. 'Only reform could avert irresistible pressures for legislation at Westminster – under the rights explicity reserved by Section 75 of the Government of Ireland Act, 1920 – intervening in Irish affairs'. But, he added significantly, 'none of us wanted that'. He did, however, point out Northern Ireland's financial dependence on Westminster, and warned that if O'Neill were overthrown 'for no other reason than opposition to his reform measures, and if he were replaced by a more extremist leadership, a new situation could arise in which Westminster's inhibitions about taking some of the measures pressed upon us would disappear'.[6] But there was as yet no clear indication of what the loss of inhibition on Westminster's part would mean in political terms.

O'Neill was presented with a package of reforms, including housing allocation, the replacement of Londonderry corporation by a development commission, reform of local government and local franchise and the amendment of the Special Powers Act. Grievances were to be investigated and an ombudsman appointed. His reflection on that meeting, that his more inflexible colleagues were 'forced to agree' to these reforms and that 'it would have ... been more dignified if we had been able to make them our proposals' revealed both the extent and limitations of British involvement in this crisis. A British government could 'force' reforms on a Unionist premier, but only at the expense of compromising his political position both in his party and among the Unionist population as a whole. But if the British government was reluctant to assume direct responsibility for the government of Northern Ireland then it must not deprive its 'moderate' Unionist prime minister of his bargaining power both within his party and with the civil rights leaders. Yet any failure to press O'Neill would give an impression that Britain was not, in the event, all that concerned about the minority position in the north of Ireland. It is doubtful if O'Neill's government could have survived the pressures from Ian Paisley and his followers, now convinced, and convincing others, that the real aim of the NICRA was the destruction of Unionism. But a Unionist government, now openly prodded along by Westminster, had very few cards to play in any political bargaining process: why should the civil rights movement deal with O'Neill when he was clearly no longer master in his own house, to use a phrase increasingly employed by O'Neill's hard-line opponents?

In January 1969 the 'People's Democracy', a student radical group, organised a march from Belfast to Derry which was attacked by Unionists, with the connivance, and in some cases the support of the police that were supposed to escort it. This incident undermined any goodwill that the November reforms had generated, and revealed how street politics could damage an already fragile Unionist government. In February O'Neill called an election, but failed to strengthen his position, and in April he was replaced by James Chichester-Clark. By now the Labour government had established a Northern Ireland cabinet committee, including leading figures in the administration, James Callaghan, Roy Jenkins, Denis Healey, Richard Crossman and Lord Gardiner, the government's senior legal adviser. And it was increasingly acknowledged that Northern Irish politics might now come to serious disorder on the streets, in which case the Unionist government could legitimately ask the British government to intervene to restore order. But there was little serious preparation made for this eventuality, perhaps because it was such a hard one for any British cabinet to contemplate; after all, not even the more experienced (in Irish terms) government of 1922 viewed direct involvement in the affairs of Northern Ireland with anything but apprehension. Callaghan reported that if it came to intervention, he had only 'a very small staff'. In April 1969 Callaghan pointed out that if troops were used then Britain could not be responsible without assuming responsibility for Northern Ireland but, Crossman wrote, 'of course I thought we were bluffing. I thought that if a crisis did come and the troops went in we couldn't throw Chichester-Clark out and we would find ourselves supporting the Orangemen in Northern Ireland'.[7]

The use of troops was resisted to the end; but the need came in August 1969 when disorder broke out, first in Derry and then Belfast and then in other areas of Northern Ireland, which the RUC could not control or suppress. Stormont had warned London that the army might have to act in aid of the civil power if violence became unmanageable. But London insisted that all local resources must be exhausted, and demonstrably exhausted, before it could contemplate military intervention. On the night of 14 August the destruction of property and the death of six people indicated that local resources were indeed exhausted. Only when the army established an effective presence in Belfast on 16 August was peace restored. This intervention, small at first, and with a slightly make-believe atmosphere as British troops drove to Derry observing every traffic signal on the way, was the turning point for the Northern Ireland crisis. It made the crisis one for Britain and British politics as well; but it was one that could be interpreted in two ways, at any rate in August 1969. The crisis continued to bear the characteristics of its earlier 'British' phase, with the emphasis placed on the implementation of long overdue reforms on the lines of the British polity itself; but it now bore an increasingly menacing 'historical' character, with those familiar spectres – familiar at least to earlier experiences of British political generations – of communal violence, sectarian war cries, the flaunting of provocative symbols and flags, Orange and Green. It was this latter consideration that prompted Callaghan and Healey to remind the cabinet on 18 August that 'our whole interest was to work through the Protestant government. The Protestants are the majority and we can't afford to alienate them as well as the Catholics and find ourselves ruling Northern Ireland as a colony'.[8]

Britain had to 'work through' the Unionists; or as the *New Statesman* put it, the British government had placed the 'Stormont regime on probation as to its civil activities and at the same time stripped it of its primary responsibility for the maintenance of order'. And while it admitted that the Catholic minority 'will never support the Stormont regime', there was 'a chance it can be persuaded to respect its British probation officer'.[9] The cabinet, for its part, spoke of its own intervention in terms of a 'complete take over'.[10] *The Economist* declared ruefully that 'Britain is once again up to the neck in the Irish question'.[11] But Britain still preferred the option of declaring that:

Every citizen of Northern Ireland is entitled to the same equality of treatment and freedom from discrimination as obtains in the rest of the United Kingdom, irrespective of political views or religion[12] and supporting a Unionist government in making good this aspiration. Substantial reforms were indeed initiated. But Northern Ireland between 1969 and 1971 was in an intensely political phase, with major new shifts in politics taking place, as the Unionist government's loss of touch with its popular following, and Catholic disillusionment with the continuing 'probationary' Stormont government, clearly indicated. All this was noticed but not remarked upon, by the British government, including the new Conservative government elected in June 1970, which was content to follow its predecessors and hope that 'reform' would act as a substitute for further, and more radical, intervention in the affairs of Northern Ireland.

II

The British desire to avoid deeper commitment to the politics of Northern Ireland only drew it more radically into those affairs in the end; and an understanding of the British dimension of the Ulster Question is vital to an understanding of the events that shook Northern Ireland between 1970 and 1972, culminating in the fall of Stormont and the creation of a power-sharing executive which lasted for a brief period in 1974. Indeed, it is no exaggeration to say that the Ulster Question would have taken a very different (but by no means necessarily a more benign) shape had not British government set the limits and possibilities to Irish politics. Britain's desire to minimise its role resulted in the establishment of a military presence as an essential part of keeping the peace, but one that was set in a rapidly decaying political context. The very presence of the army, moreover, was not seen in Northern Ireland, as it was in Britain, as that of a neutral peace-keeping force, a kind of military guarantor of civilian reforms. On the contrary. Protestants found its presence puzzling and disturbing, a sign of their novel and much resented political disadvantage. Catholics could not help but recall memories of this army's traditional role as an old enemy, especially when IRA harassment of the army provoked retaliation which confirmed those Republican voices now prophesying war.

Between the summer of 1970 and the winter of 1971 the army was already a political factor in Northern Ireland; the recovery of Unionism was to confirm that political role.

The Unionist government, by now humiliated and damaged, seemed to find a new lease of life when the vigorous and active Brian Faulkner replaced James Chichester-Clark as prime minister in March 1971. Faulkner offered the Social Democratic and Labour Party, founded in 1970 and representing Catholic opinion, four new parliamentary committees to deal with social services and the like, two of which at least would have SDLP representatives as salaried chairmen. Favourable initial reaction was replaced by suspicion; but in any event the crisis was rapidly moving towards one that involved one of the central aspects of the state of Northern Ireland: security. Faulkner was prime minister; his main security forces were, however, British troops; and when Faulkner finally opted for an internment swoop against the IRA, now a revitalised force, in August 1971 he inevitably brought the British government into the Ulster crisis, for that government was ultimately responsible for Stormont, and of course for its own army.

Internment was, in purely military terms, successful;[13] but allegations of indiscriminate arrest and brutality, especially in interrogation of suspects, brought a storm of protest from Catholic representatives. British public opinion was inclined to rally to its much abused army; but liberal opinion in the press was sickened, not only by internment, but by the fact that Britain was being held responsible for it. The government established an inquiry to take the edge off criticism; but it did not address itself to the central problem of internment, which was: would any military success be undermined by the political reaction in the minority in Northern Ireland; and if internment was then to be only half-hearted, would it inflict final defeat on the damaged but still intact IRA?

The SDLP had already extricated itself from any further dealings with Stormont as a result of the army's shooting of two Catholic youths in Derry on 8 July; now the pressure was intensified, and in January 1972 a civil rights march, in defiance of a government ban on marches (but not on meetings) resulted in the reckless shooting by the army of thirteen civilians. Without the illegal parade there would have been no 'Bloody Sunday'; but by now many Catholics no longer regarded Stormont's bans and laws as in any way legal, or deserving of respect: internment had demonstrated that Unionist law prevailed in Northern Ireland.

The events of 'Bloody Sunday' rang around the world; as John Hume's biographer put it, Hume's home 'was like a railway station for days to come, as the world's Press, and the entire Irish establishment, Government and Opposition, beat a path to his door'.[14] Just as in the internment controversy, the British government was obliged to act as judge and jury on the behaviour of the army and, indirectly, on that of the Unionist government. Yet another commission was set up to investigate the events of 'Bloody Sunday', and what Britain regarded as a fair inquiry and report was inevitably dismissed in Catholic circles as humbug and hypocrisy, and in Protestant circles as weakness in the face of the Catholic threat to the state. In March 1972 Brian Faulkner made the inevitable visit to Downing Street to give an account of his stewardship, expecting to discuss matters of constitutional reform, such as a bill of rights. But the reform option had at last, in the British view, run its course. Faulkner was faced with Heath's insistence that security be removed from Stormont's competence; that internment must end; that a referendum would be held on the border (as a sop to Unionism); but that the government must consult with the Labour opposition about efforts to create a 'community government'; and that a secretary of state for Northern Ireland would be appointed. All this left Faulkner with not even the shreds of authority; and his decision to resign, on the grounds that Northern Ireland was not a 'coconut colony' followed almost instantly. On 24 March Heath accepted Faulkner's resignation, and London resumed direct control for the affairs of Northern Ireland after a gap of some 50 years: on 30 March the Northern Ireland (Temporary Provisions) Act suspended Stormont for one year, and placed a secretary of state, William Whitelaw, over the province.

The fall of Stormont was a major turning point in the Northern Ireland Question. It marked the final stage in the dismantling of the Anglo-Irish settlements of 1920–21. This went unrecognised by the British, who regarded the suspension of governing institutions in Northern Ireland as only temporary. But the British way of politics, based on compromise and bargaining, could be applied to Northern Ireland only with great difficulty; for any bargains struck by a British secretary of state must inevitably touch the sensitive nerve of the Northern Ireland problem: the deep division in the population, a division that took different and modern forms which so excited Marxist observers of the scene, but which was not amenable to the forces of bargaining: Protestants suspected that their privileges, and indeed their very existence, could be bargained away, admittedly with the best will and intentions on the British part; Catholics were anxious to press home the advantages they had gained so far, and would be ever watchful for any Conservative reluctance to stand up to those who were their allies in the past. Meanwhile the army's anti-terrorist initiative was allowed to run down, and any gains won by internment were forfeited, while the political losses still remained on the balance sheet.[15]

The Conservatives had indeed played a significant role in the shaping of the Ulster crisis, even when in opposition. Harold Wilson's jibe that they 'did nothing in particular and did it very well'[16] contained an important, if unacknowledged, element of truth; for the failure of the Conservatives to lend any hope or comfort to the Unionists in their dilemmas in 1969–70 revealed that the party had no wish to revive its Unionist past. Now, in government, they were under pressure from the Labour opposition to admit that there was an 'Irish dimension' to the Northern Ireland crisis, and that Northern Ireland was not an integral part of the United Kingdom like Kent or Surrey.

Following internment Wilson declared that it was 'impossible to conceive of an effective long-term solution which is not in some way directed to finding a means of achieving the aspiration towards a United Ireland'.[17] The Dublin government for its part had moved towards at least a verbal declaration of the need for acknowledgement of a role for the south in northern affairs, and the word partition returned to Irish politics, however superficially these emotions were felt. Now the Conservative government, in its search for new institutions in Northern Ireland was willing to acknowledge that indeed there was a Catholic aspiration towards unity, however long term for the most part, and that Dublin might be involved in this in some constructive way.

This British view, like Gladstone's view of the Irish Question in 1886 helped define the question in significant ways, and push it in directions that were to have much influence on its character. The British government undertook a political initiative to bring together in a power-sharing executive those groups in Northern Ireland that could be defined as 'moderate': Unionists led by Brian Faulkner; the Social Democratic and Labour Party; and the non-sectarian Alliance Party. But the British perception of an 'Irish Dimension' to the Ulster crisis was now given a tangible acknowledgement in the Sunningdale Agreement of December 1973, which followed closely upon the governmental arrangements in Northern Ireland itself.

The new constitution was, on the face of it, a bold and hopeful experiment. But it reflected the underlying ambiguities of British policy in Ireland. Its advantage for Britain was in its distancing effect: it once more thrust upon Ulstermen the primary responsibility of governing themselves. But Westminster retained security powers; which might have to be used to defend the new executive, and which therefore might draw Britain back into the centre of political controversy. It allowed Dublin an ill-defined role in Northern Ireland affairs, for a 'Council of Ireland' was insisted upon by Dublin and the SDLP at the Sunningdale Conference as an essential part of the new arrangements. This rallied strong Unionist opposition, but did little to help the Catholic minority. Above all, the new executive, however worthy, was an imposed settlement, imposed by the British government. Yet it lacked the necessary political and public support in Britain that might be called upon if Britain's will were to prevail. The British concept of a settlement still tended to be that the worst was over once the ink of the signatories was dry on the page; and the experiment in government was not underpinned by supportive social and economic policies.

It was easy for more extreme Unionists – and those not so extreme – to allege that the Conservatives had 'betrayed Ulster'; the imposition of the hated Council of Ireland was to them proof enough of the betrayal. But Britain found all this wholly unreasonable; and in any case Heath was soon embroiled in other problems as he confronted a second, and more serious, strike by the National Union of Mineworkers in February 1974, a strike which provoked him into calling a general election on the slogan of 'who governs Britain?' This election enabled opponents of Sunningdale to treat the campaign as one in which the question was 'who governs Northern Ireland?' It offered opposition Unionists the chance to launch their assault on the power-sharing executive; and a United Ulster Unionist front swept the board, taking all of the twelve Westminster seats.

The defeat of the Conservative government and the incoming Labour administration's declaration of its commitment to the power-sharing executive brought only a breathing space for the experiment; Merlyn Rees, the Northern Ireland secretary, declared on 4 April that 'our policies will be fairly based on those of our predecessors in office'.[18] Within a few weeks the government's resolve was put to the test, and found wanting, when the Ulster Workers' Council organised a political strike against the executive. No newly elected British government, faced with economic and social problems in what it thought of as 'home' would have had much stomach for a major conflict in Northern Ireland; and the defence of the Northern Ireland executive would have required a greater political and military commitment than any British government was prepared to undertake. Rees admitted that 'there was no question of asking the army to take over the province'; what he sought instead was 'some action to show moderate opinion that the government and the Executive had the will to govern and were capable of influencing events, something to retain their credibility'.[19]

Despite the failure of 'moderation', the British were still committed to the search for a moderate solution. This was not a means of avoiding the issue in Northern Ireland (though it offered that useful possibility also); it was the only way open to a government that was 'British', whatever its political complexion. Now that British parties had placed themselves above the party feud in Ireland, now that Labour and Conservatives alike had distanced themselves from the contending groups there, there was no other option available. This is not a criticism of British intentions; the traditional saving grace of British politics – its belief in the middle ground – might indeed be imparted to Ireland with a great deal of profit. But the tactics that this course involved had serious consequences for political conditions in Northern Ireland. Security was inevitably part of the search for moderation, and this meant in effect allowing the IRA to wrest the initiative from the army, which was now given the unenviable task of 'holding the line'; this was naturally taken by the IRA and its supporters as a sign that terrorism was effective, that the bullet won victories over the British and the security forces; this in turn increased IRA prestige.[20] It also provoked the escalation of the fierce and brutal Protestant violence against (mainly innocent) Roman Catholics. There was no reason why a consistent security policy, firmly based within the law, should not have been pursued along with the search for new political options; and had these options met with success, then indeed security policy might have been appropriately modified. But the sense of drift and aimlessness that pervaded British policy in Northern Ireland in the 1970s was not conducive to the effective conduct of security.

Moreover, British perception of the Ulster crisis in the 1970s was not calculated to lessen Unionist fears about the degree of commitment that Britain felt to the Union. During the crisis over the Ulster workers' strike Harold Wilson appeared on television to denounce 'these people' as 'spongers' on 'Westminster and British democracy', words which he later described as 'open to criticism'.[21] And which were, in any case, directed at what Wilson's biographer, Ben Pimlott, described as 'mainland voters, to reassure them, not to Loyalists'.[22] Following the fall of the executive Labour took up direct rule unenthusiastically, with hints (that were perhaps leaks) in the British press that the government was considering 'withdrawal' from the province. The distancing of Great Britain from Northern Ireland was vividly illustrated in November 1974 when, in the wake of an IRA bombing outrage in Birmingham, the government rushed through Westminster a 'Prevention of Terrorism Act' which, a Labour cabinet minister admitted privately, was 'equivalent to banishing British citizens'[23] to Northern Ireland which was – supposedly – part of the United Kingdom.

It is hardly surprising that the remainder of the Labour government's life witnessed a policy of what Wilson admitted must have seemed a 'negative almost defeatist' character, with 'no new proposal for the future of the province'. Wilson declared that 'no solution could be imposed from across the water'.[24] This was a realistic admission, although it avoided the question of whether or not the power-sharing executive might have been better supported 'from across the water'; but it was followed by further moves by the government that only served to make Northern Ireland politics more tense and uneasy. A convention of Ulster parties was called, not to get a 'solution', but as in 1917, to demonstrate that it was Ireland, and not Britain, that stood in the way of solutions. But while the convention was sitting, the government made a truce with the IRA in February 1975 on the basis, as one British civil servant put it, that 'the paramilitary figures of today are the politicians of tomorrow'. This amounted to an almost formal recognition of the IRA, undermined the SDLP, and provoked the profound distrust of Unionists; it also did little for army and police morale. Civilian casualties remained high during the 'truce'; but the British response to Catholic and Protestant demands for more effective security measures was that 'crises come and crises go. This is just one of many which we do not recognise as a crisis'. When Rees argued that a British withdrawal would mean violence 'that . . . would inevitably lap over into Britain'[25] his concern, though well founded, seemed to many Ulstermen to indicate a characteristically British order of priorities.

The ceasefire may have been an attempt to divide and thus weaken the IRA;[26] but, as Rees put it disarmingly it was 'a long way from a genuine cessation of violence'.[27] And when the convention failed to come up with new or workable proposals, Wilson contented himself with musing on the possibility of a 'Lancaster House type conference' such as had considered the Rhodesian problem, but whose real purpose, however, would be 'to impress the Westminster parties with the "insufferability" of the Northern Ireland policitians and to stop the Ulster Unionists making common cause with the Tories'. The Northern Ireland secretary, Merlyn Rees, objected, and Wilson now called all the Westminster parties successively to Downing Street, supposedly for an open-ended conference on Northern Ireland, but, in his biographer Austen Morgan's opinion, really to associate the other parties with the Government's failure to create an internal solution.[28] The replacement of Rees by Roy Mason began a period of quiescence in British policy which reflected the British inability to devise new policies, and their understandable desire to let well enough alone. In the spring of 1979 the James Callaghan government committed itself to increasing Westminster representation of Northern Ireland; but with the Labour government stumbling towards its demise, this proved to be the last item of its Northern Ireland legacy; it was also the last time since the nineteenth century that an Irish vote brought down a British administration: Gerry Fitt MP aroused by the government's deal with the Ulster Unionists, voted against it and occasioned the government's resignation.

III

The fall of the Labour government at the hands of an Irish vote must provoke some reflections on the Northern Ireland Question in British politics since 1969, and in particular on the role of the Labour Party. This was, after all, the party that had deep roots in Wales and Scotland; which had evolved a devolution policy for Wales and Scotland in the 1970s; and which might have been expected to view the Northern Ireland problem through somewhat different perspectives, especially since the heady days of 1965–69 when the Labour government's backbenchers, and Harold Wilson himself, were involving themselves as never before in the affairs of the province. Yet the Labour Party held no full-scale debate on Northern Ireland at its party conferences between 1969 and 1981, and no discussion at all in 1973 and 1975.[29] There was some advantage in this as far as Northern Ireland was concerned, since British party political debates on Irish matters were not marked by any deep understanding of the issues. But this left the way open to the more colourful interpretations placed on the Northern Ireland crisis by the more extreme left, in which Northern Ireland was seen as the last outpost of the capitalist British Empire, and (paradoxically) as the first advance guard of the overthrowing of the capitalist system in the whole British Isles, and possibly even the world. These ideas were in one sense irrelevant; but they gained a wider currency than might be expected, and helped the IRA and its political front Sinn Fein to coordinate its propaganda on the lines of a 'third world' struggle against imperialist forces. 'Socialism' was somehow linked with the ending of partition. And no-one on the Left believed that the problem in Northern Ireland had anything to do with religion.[30]

It would be wrong to see Labour's distancing of itself from Northern Ireland as a conspiracy to withdraw from the province, though Harold Wilson's own inclination was for withdrawal, and it seems that only Dublin's fear of the consequenses dissuaded him; at a Cabinet meeting during the Loyalist Workers' strike withdrawal was seriously considered, with Tony Benn noting philosophically that 'of course, if that got out, it would precipitate bloodshed but we felt we simply had to do it'.[31] With this radical option abandoned, the Party now sought a Northern Ireland policy that would please its own left wing at a time when the party was seeking desperately to recover from the catastrophe of its defeat in the 1979 general election, and when unity was all important. Thus in 1981 Labour's official Irish policy became one of 'unity by consent'.[32] It is doubtful if this can be dignified with the name of policy, since policies in politics are means by which realisable ends are to be achieved. These were empty words, perhaps involving some danger to the Ulster crisis in that they aroused Protestant fears and IRA hopes, but words of more relevance to the Labour Party's needs as a British party in pursuit of government rather than to the realities of the Irish predicament. They offered no immediate relief to the embattled Catholic minority in the north. Like Labour's devolution strategy in the whole United Kingdom in the 1970s, it was motivated by party political concerns. But this of course could have an effect on Northern Ireland politics, and the prospect of the implementation of this vague, but disconcerting, aim opened up new and trouble-some anxieties in the province.

The Conservative Party also disengaged itself from too close an association with its former Unionist allies, if in a rather more characteristically pragmatic style. The Thatcher government, elected in 1979, commenced with a series of intergovernmental meetings, 'summits' held on a 'continuing basis' between Dublin and London.[33] This process was given a greater urgency by the IRA hunger strike of May–August 1981, and especially by the death of its leader, Bobby Sands, which landed Britain once more in the forefront (and in many places in the dock) of world opinion. The hunger strike demonstrated to Ulster Unionists that the Conservative government had a determined face when it came to resisting the pressure of Republican propaganda and self-sacrifice: the murders of Airey Neave and Lord Mountbatten were hardly calculated to soften its response, whatever the reaction amongst Nationalists in Northern Ireland. But it did not permanently damage relations between Dublin and London, despite southern politicians' appeals for a more flexible policy. In November 1981 Mrs Thatcher met the Republic's premier, Garret Fitzgerald, at Downing Street, and the decision was made to establish an Anglo-Irish Intergovernmental Council to give institutional form to the relationship between Britain and Ireland.

This process was interrupted by two political developments, one in Northern Ireland and one in international relations. In April 1982 the newly elected Fianna Fail government of Charles Haughey watched with scepticism yet another attempt to find agreement within the north as the Northern Ireland secretary, James Prior, outlined his proposals for an elected assembly of 78 members presided over by an executive of 13 members, who would have control over all the affairs of the province that used to be exercised by the old Stormont legislature. 70 per cent of assembly members must agree on the form of executive, and then it would ask the British government to transfer these powers (everything except defence, foreign affairs and taxes) to the new executive. The SDLP regarded this as guaranteeing an inbuilt Protestant hegemony, despite Prior's concession that if there were less than 70 per cent agreement on some subjects, they could still be transferred if there was sufficient Protestant–Catholic consensus. But this would require Catholic representatives to work hard to frustrate the development of a Protestant parliament; and the concept of 'rolling devolution' worried Protestants, who feared that it might roll them out of the United Kingdom. The Prior initiative, moreover, excluded the SDLP's essential 'Irish dimension'; and so the various parties went into the elections for the assembly in November 1982 with apathy rather than hope. But there was a surprise in store: Sinn Fein won one third of the Catholic vote on the slogan of the gun and the ballot; and Ian Paisley's Democratic Unionists polled as many votes (but won less seats) than the Official Unionists. The SDLP and Sinn Fein refused to take their seats; and the long anticipated victory of 'moderates' in Ulster politics was as elusive as ever.

The victory of moderation was hardly any easier to achieve in the wider world. Between May and July 1982 Anglo-Irish relations touched a new depth of estrangement as the Irish government refused to follow the rest of the EEC and impose an embargo on Argentine trade. There was also much blustering in Dublin about 'colonialism'. But although the Falklands war placed the joint study programme in abeyance, its advantages could not be ignored. British policy lacked coherence, but at least two motives could reassert themselves: the need to create a better atmosphere in the north, and especially to recover the ground lost by constitutional nationalism to Sinn Fein in the aftermath of the hunger strike; and the opportunity to make sure that the Northern Ireland Problem was shared with those in Dublin who claimed the right to be consulted, but who seemed inclined to shirk the responsibilities involved in consultation, especially in the areas of security and the extradition of suspects to the United Kingdom. In December 1982 Mrs Thatcher declared to one of her chief civil servants that 'if we get back next time . . . I think I would like to do something about Ireland'.[34]

The British government did not move towards any new departure in a linear fashion. On the contrary, between May 1983 and 1985 the main initiatives in the region of new ideas about the future of Northern Ireland, and its relations with the south, took place in Ireland itself, especially in the New Ireland Forum in

Dublin in which constitutional nationalists took stock of their position in the last quarter of the twentieth century, and concluded that while Ulster Unionism was indeed guilty at the bar of history, it could be forgiven its sins. Less forgivable was the alleged role of the British government, first in partitioning Ireland in 1920, and then, since 1969, indulging only in 'crisis management'. There was also some wishful thinking about the prospects of an Ireland without a British security presence. But one item in the Forum Report's recommendations was to have a more significant role in the near future:

> Under joint authority, the London and Dublin governments would have equal responsibility for all aspects of the government of Northern Ireland.

This proposal was not accepted by the British government. But its importance lay in preparing the ground for a phase in Anglo-Irish relations when the 'Irish Dimension' was again regarded as an essential part of any new political initiative. As one Westminster politician said, 'for decades Nationalists have been saying "Brits out" – but joint authority is by definition "Brits in" '.[35] Moreover the possibility of some greater degree of cooperation between Dublin and London meant that the spectre of British withdrawal from Northern Ireland which (whatever their public pronouncements) haunted all responsible southern Irish political parties, would be dismissed: 'Brits in' had real advantages for the Republic as well.[36]

The Forum Report was debated in the House of Commons on 2 July 1984; and it was met with a welcoming, but guarded, response by James Prior, some criticism from Conservative backbenchers and a predictable reaction from Labour, now more than ever convinced that a united Ireland was in the best interests of the people of Northern Ireland, but still unsure how this might be reconciled with 'consent'. In November 1984 the Irish and British governments met in the second summit of the Anglo-Irish Intergovernmental Council, and agreed on a statement full of good intentions about security, community relations and the rest of the ingredients of the Northern Ireland problem; but in a press conference immediately afterwards the British prime minister declared that a unified Ireland was 'out' and so was confederation of two states and joint authority. All this was perfectly in line with the talks just concluded; its style, however, was very much at variance with the attempt being made by ministers on both sides to talk to each other in reasonable terms.

But the dismissal of the Forum options did not mean that the British and Irish governments were left with no other common ground. The government, after all, had just survived a murderous bombing attack on the Conservative Party conference hotel in Brighton; its aftermath was hardly the appropriate moment to make key decisions, since these might be interpreted as in some sense inspired by or forced on the cabinet by the IRA. Moreover the summer of 1985 saw the publication of yet more positive constitutional proposals, in the form of a Penguin Special written by two Northern Irish academics, and a joint report by the Liberals and the Social Democratic Party. Informed public opinion in Britain was becoming used to the idea that something had to be done. On 15 November 1985 something was done: Mrs Thatcher and Dr Garret Fitzgerald met at Hillsborough Castle outside Belfast in the third of their series of meetings between heads of government. There they signed a firm and formal agreement whose aims were to promote 'peace and stability in Northern Ireland'; and to help, 'reconcile the two main traditions in Ireland'; to create a new climate of friendship and cooperation between the people of Great Britain and Ireland; and to improve 'co-operation in combating terrorism'. The agreement allowed Dublin a consultative role in Northern Ireland affairs; it re-affirmed the majority's right to decide on the constitutional future of Northern Ireland; it promised financial help from the United States of America to foster industrial development in the north. This appeared laudable; but there was to Unionists a suspicious ambiguity in the language used in the agreement. The agreement affirmed the right of the majority in Northern Ireland; but the words used were that it recognised 'the present wish of a majority of the people of Northern Ireland is for no change', and promised that 'if in the future a majority . . . clearly wish for and formally consent to the establishment of a united Ireland', the Dublin and London governments would 'introduce and support in their respective Parliaments legislation to give effect to that wish'.[37]

These words seemed to imply, to Unionists, an unhealthy and unseemly concern to facilitate a united Ireland; they read rather like the hopes of a legatee who was inquiring perhaps too eagerly and assiduously about the health of a relative whose prospects (or the lack of them) for survival were of real and immediate interest.

That the agreement should be the work of a Conservative government was particularly bitter gall for Unionists, whose suspicion of Labour was innate, but who, as Harold McCusker put it 'in my most pessimistic moments . . . never believed that the agreement would deliver me, in the context that it has, into the hands of those who for 15 years have murdered personal friends, political associates, and hundreds of my constituents'.[38] Unionist bewilderment was increased because they had watched with satisfaction the outburst of British patriotism aroused by the Falklands war; now they discovered that this patriotism was for 'home' consumption only. It was one thing to send the fleet in style to the South Atlantic to confront what the popular press and parliament saw as a 'tinpot dictator'. It was quite another to order troops to take their chance on what *The Economist*, in its anger, called the 'mean streets' of Belfast, 'made meaner by Protestant bigotry'.[39]

Despite Unionist astonishment, the government's Northern Ireland policy did not represent a sudden and inexplicable change of front, but the crystallisation of ideas and notions that had been canvassed and considered since 1981. The Hillsborough Agreement still excluded what Mrs Thatcher, in her remarkable 'out, out, out' speech denounced in November 1984: a united Ireland, confederation and joint authority. But it must be seen in the context of intergovernmental summits, the Forum Report and the fact that some kind of Dublin involvement in the affairs of Northern Ireland had made its way into the political agenda. Meetings between British and Irish government ministers and their senior civil servants were, after all, meetings of like minds in a general sense: minds that pondered upon the intractable north, and sought ways forward, could find common ground in private conference where they could not in public politics. The problem might be that, as Lord Fitt put it in characteristic style, agreements that looked reasonable in Britain were not acceptable in Ireland, because 'the more unreasonable you are over there the more success you are guaranteed electorally'.[40]

In Britain, matters looked different. There 'reason' prevailed. The Hillsborough Agreement was received almost uncritically; and senior figures from the Labour and Conservative (and other) Parties added their weight to the front benches. Only the far right of the Conservative Party and the far left of the Labour Party denounced it, as on the one hand a sell-out to nationalism, and on the other a rejection of the United Ireland solution favoured by Benn and his like. The lack of 'reason' in Ireland provoked a hostile reaction in Great Britain, where the *Economist*, for its part, fulminated against those who were 'biting a hand that is feeding them more kindness than they deserve', and took to task those loyalists who seemed to think that 'mainland Britain' could be exploited to 'send British taxpayers millions to pay the unemployed swollen by anti-Catholic discrimination – with no corresponding obligation of tolerance or compromise in return'.

This generally uncritical, and in some quarters rabid, support in Britain deserves analysis. The chief immediate beneficiary of the Agreement was Britain. For it put Britain right in the eyes of the world, and of her chief critics: she was seen to be doing something to stand up to Unionism, and she was implementing policy in the context of the whole British Isles: Dublin and London were now talking to each other on better terms than ever before. The benefits for Northern Ireland were less immediately apparent. But it was undeniable that if Northern Irish constitutional nationalism were to be fatally undermined by the challenge of Provisional Sinn Fein, then the whole island of Ireland, and Great Britain as well, would sink deeper into crisis.

The most vociferous critics were found among the Protestants of Northern Ireland. The Unionist response, with the withdrawal of Unionist MPs from Westminster, protest meetings, parades, gang warfare, strikes and non-cooperation suggested that the Unionist people were in revolt. Yet the terms of the Agreement were such that, while they aroused Unionist fury, they did not in fact place the Union in such jeopardy that Unionists must feel that they had no alternative save the ultimate sanction: a self-destructive rebellion against the British government. For the

Hillsborough Agreement held two coded messages for the people of Northern Ireland as a whole. It advised the Nationalists not to change their allegiance to the SDLP (or to change it back, if need be). And it advised the Unionists to change, and adapt their politics to the new circumstances of Anglo-Irish relations.

The final outcome of the Hillsborough Agreement is could not course be predicted by anyone; but its reception in British political circles and the British media indicated that, while the Irish Question might divide Irishman from Irishman, Unionist from Nationalist, its capacity to divide the British political world was utterly exhausted. Few in Great Britain could feel any more affinity with Ulster Protestants than they could with Roman Catholics.[41] At the end of the two-day debate on the Agreement, the motion approving it was carried by 473 votes to 47. This was one of the largest majorities on a division in parliamentary history. In 1885 Gladstone was convinced that a bipartisan approach to the Irish Question on the part of the British political parties would offer the best chance of a solution to the Irish Question. Now that belief was to be put to the test.

5

QUESTIONS AND ANSWERS, 1986–1996: WAR AND PEACE IN A DECADE OF TROUBLES

I

Between the Anglo-Irish Agreement of 1985 and the Anglo-Irish 'Framework' document of February 1995 British policy in Northern Ireland achieved a dramatic breakthrough, one hardly predictable in the immediate aftermath of the 1985 initiative. The British government hoped, through the Anglo-Irish Agreement, to involve the Dublin government more closely, and more constructively, in the crisis management of the North; and also, more immediately, to mobilise Dublin in improved security cooperation. Indeed, much of the pre-Agreement discussions were dedicated to the question of a more coordinated anti-terrorist strategy, including easier extradition facilities between the Republic and Great Britain.[1] There was also the hope that, in the longer term, Dublin's role as advocate of the Roman Catholics' interests in Northern Ireland would significantly affect the Sinn Fein vote; and that, if Unionist protests against the Agreement failed, then they would emerge as sadder and wiser people, more willing to consider compromise. Above all, a new atmosphere would be created in Anglo-Irish relations, with the two states acting in partnership and thus transcending the narrow ground of the deeply contested politics of Northern Ireland.

The first four years of the new era failed to live up to these expectations. Almost immediately the British prime minister, Margaret Thatcher, began to draw the conclusion that, as she put it in a conversation with the Republic's Taoiseach, Dr Garret Fitzgerald (in which, as he puts it, she 'jumped around from point to point'), 'You've got the glory and I've got the problems'. She had been told that she was treacherous and had betrayed the Unionists; she must reassure them. She feared that dissent in her own party and Ulster Unionist protests would increase. There must be 'visible action on security'.[2] All this revealed a Mrs Thatcher very different from the 'iron lady' depicted in the British media. The problem, she went on, was that Unionists would only hear what they wanted to hear. 'It was no good saying things with an English voice: Irish voices must come in and help'. In particular, the notion that the Agreement amounted to joint authority must be dispelled, and, clutching at straws, she hoped that the Irish claim that the Agreement was the nearest thing to joint authority would quash the Unionists's claim that it *was* joint authority.[3]

In Northern Irish political terms, the strength of the Agreement lay in the fact that it was difficult to overthrow; for, unlike the power-sharing Sunningdale experiment, it offered no tangible, local target to Unionist dissidents. There was no local constituency in which protest could be registered, and Unionist non-cooperation could be regarded as almost a bonus, relegating Northern Ireland politicians to their own back yard. To be sure, there were Unionist demonstrations on the streets, and many ugly incidents; but there was no loss of life as a result of these protests, and the RUC were able to weather the storm. But, at a deeper level, the Agreement posed two major problems for the British government. One was that, having signed a document which pleased the Nationalists of Northern Ireland, or most of them at any rate, the Government might now find it imperative, as Mrs Thatcher herself put it, to reassure the Unionists.[4] The delicacy of this position was revealed when the Northern Ireland Secretary, Tom King, made a speech in Brussels on 3 December 1985 in which he alleged that, notwithstanding aspirations for sovereignty over Northern Ireland, the prime minister of the Republic had accepted that for all practical purposes and in perpetuity there never would be a united Ireland. This drew a storm of protests from Dublin, and the row took some time to defuse.[5] British policy seemed yet again on the road to conciliating one side at the expense of the other, and then reversing the process.

A second major problem with the Agreement, and one that seemed to threaten its spirit, if not its letter, was the security issue. This was the specifically British agenda, and one that, in British perception, was incompatible with the Irish government's desire to ensure a speedy reform of the judicial system in Northern Ireland itself. The British were concerned with extradition of terrorist suspects, and expected the Irish parliament to move quickly to ease the process; the Irish government felt that it would find this difficult unless the British reformed the so-called 'Diplock' system in the North, by which terrorist cases were tried by a judge acting without a jury. These issues were not necessarily linked together, but political expediency dictated otherwise; as Dr Fitzgerald put it, 'this reform . . . would have helped us in our difficult task of getting the extradition legislation through the Dáil in the autumn of that year'.[6] The extradition question was eventually taken up by the Fianna Fail government of Charles Haughey, but under the shadow of deep disquiet felt by many at the British legal system's handling of an appeal made against their convictions by the 'Birmingham Six' following a bomb attack in that city in 1974. On 1 December 1987 Haughey steered through an extradition act by 78–22 votes, with 62 abstentions, but the British government declared itself disappointed with amendments giving the Irish attorney-general the right to form an opinion on whether or not to accept the extradition warrant and stipulating that the extradited person could only be tried for the offence detailed in the extradition papers. What were described as 'intense diplomatic exchanges' took place just before the Dáil vote, and Mrs Thatcher claimed that the amendments made the United Kingdom 'the least favoured nation in Europe' in seeking extradition from Ireland. The Ulster Unionist Party leader, James Molyneux, described the affair as 'the most serious rift with Dublin for a decade'. This was followed by a sense of outrage in Ireland when the appeal of the Birmingham Six against their conviction was refused in January 1988.[7]

Another serious dispute developed between London and Dublin over the 'Stalker–Sampson' affair, which had its origins in the appointment of John Stalker, Deputy Chief Constable of the Greater Manchester Police, in May 1984 to lead an inquiry into allegations of a 'shoot to kill' policy by the RUC. In September 1985, Stalker presented an interim report recommending the prosecution of eleven RUC officers; but when he persisted in his request to have access to evidence (a tape recording) which he thought vital to the case, the RUC Chief Constable, Sir John Hermon, refused unless the Director of Public Prosecutions ordered otherwise. In February 1986, on receiving Stalker's report, the DPP ordered that he have access to the evidence; but Stalker was sent on 'extended leave' and replaced as the officer in charge of the investigation by the West Yorkshire Chief Constable, Colin Sampson. On 30 June, Stalker was suspended from duty while an investigation was made into his alleged association with known criminals. Not surprisingly, suspicions of 'dirty tricks' were reinforced when Stalker was cleared of the charges and reinstated in August 1986. The controversy deepened when, following Sampson's completion of the inquiry into the RUC in March 1987, the Attorney General announced that no criminal proceedings would be instituted as this would be contrary to the interests of national security. The Irish government demanded a special meeting of the Anglo-Irish Conference to consider the affair, but the Northern Ireland Secretary, Tom King, refused to disclose the details of what aspect of 'national security' lay behind the Attorney General's decision not to prosecute. The Stalker–Sampson affair strained British bi-partisanship, as the Labour Party demanded an emergency debate and a judicial inquiry, both of which were refused by the government. A motion by the Irish representatives in the European Parliament condemning the decision not to prosecute was approved by 181 votes to 51, and was a public and international acknowledgement of the suspicions aroused in the Irish government by the British handling of the case.[8]

But, much to the disappointment of Unionists, the fundamentals of the Anglo-Irish Agreement were not shaken by these cases and controversies. The Agreement held the field, partly because it was hoped that its dividends would eventually emerge; it was in any case preferable to reverting to the status quo. Dublin and

London would, broadly speaking, try to retain some cohesion in Northern Ireland policy, however much they might differ in these vexing security matters. Dublin, for its part, felt more secure with the Agreement, as they saw it, tying the British into Northern Ireland: there would be no more uncomfortable asides about a 'British withdrawal' as there were in the 1970s. London had reaped a reward in the international congratulations that showered upon it for its bold policy in making the Agreement, and would not want to forfeit this advantage, nor would it wish to break the bi-partisanship approach amongst British political parties that the Agreement exemplified: a bi-partisanship that was strained, but not in constitutional policy matters broken, when Labour criticised government security responses and expedients.

The British and Irish governments had hoped that the Anglo-Irish Agreement would prevent what they perceived as significant decline in the constitutional nationalist SDLP vote, and the corresponding increase in the Sinn Fein electoral support, following the hunger strike of 1981. The United Kingdom general election of 1987 bore this out to some extent, with the SDLP increasing their share of the vote by 3.2 per cent as against their performance in 1983, and Sinn Fein's percentage of the vote falling to 11.4 per cent as against their 1983 performance of 13.4 per cent. The non-sectarian Alliance Party won 10 per cent of the poll, while the Ulster Unionist Party gained 37.8 per cent and Ian Paisley's Democratic Unionists dropped from 20 per cent to 11.7 per cent.[9] The following September the Ulster Unionist leaders, James Molyneux and the Reverend Ian Paisley, met Tom King for 'talks about talks',[10] the first meeting between Unionist politicians and government ministers in 19 months. In November 1988, the third anniversary of the signing of the Anglo-Irish Agreement passed with only minor Unionist protests. It was clear that it had come to stay, and that it would continue to be the bedrock of British policy in Northern Ireland for the foreseeable future.

Indeed, the Agreement almost became an end in itself, despite Mrs Thatcher's (mistaken) claim that agreement over devolved government in Northern Ireland and power-sharing could 'knock out' its institutions.[11] The question remained about what it had done to help resolve the conflict in Northern Ireland. It had clearly not established Dublin–London relations on a permanently easy footing, as the controversy over the shooting of three IRA members in Gibraltar by the SAS in March 1988 demonstrated.[12] Nor had it reduced the level of violence: on the contrary, Loyalist terrorism was soon to rival, and then overtake, Republican terrorism in the 1990s. What it did achieve was the political isolation of Ulster Unionism. This was clearly, and tragically, demonstrated by the reaction in Britain following an IRA bomb attack on a Remembrance Day service in Enniskillen, Co. Fermanagh, on 8 November 1987. This atrocity provoked a wave of revulsion across Ireland, Britain and the rest of Europe, and indeed the world. But it was seen, not primarily as an assault upon Unionists, nor as an IRA gesture of contempt for their traditions, but as a personal and human tragedy of the kind that happened in Northern Ireland. Moreover, it was presented as a kind of by-product of Northern Ireland's intransigent political parties and unmovable political leaders, and especially those in the Unionist camp. Taken to its logical conclusion (which many did) the Enniskillen murders could even be blamed, in part at least, on those Unionists whose refusal to compromise had now reaped its own terrible harvest. The people slain at Enniskillen were the victims of Unionist ideology.[13]

But the Irish question in British politics had always a political dimension, in the sense that it impinged, even in an era of bipartisanship, on the British political system. The events in the post Anglo-Irish Agreement world only illustrated this point more clearly. On the one hand, British proposals for Ireland could always be presented as constitution-making, as efforts by government to find a reasonable settlement, or lay the foundations for a settlement; on the other, the state of British parties at any moment played a role in how they would react to the problem. The Conservative Party in government had, since the time of Edward Heath, reduced its commitment to the Ulster Unionists; but, even while Mrs Thatcher was enduring Unionist wrath at the Anglo-Irish Agreement, she was also displaying anxiety about dissension within her own party at what she had done. Similarly, the Labour Party in opposition in the 1980s modified its position from that of seeking a united Ireland 'by consent' (which would scarcely endear it to the Unionists), to an assurance given by Neil Kinnock in February 1992 to Molyneux and Paisley that, while this broad objective remained in view, any political talks about Northern Ireland in the event of a Labour Government being elected would not be designed to advance the cause of Irish unity.[14] The British general election of 1992 was likely to prove a closely run contest, and Unionists hoped that they might hold the balance in a hung parliament.

While these political calculations were being made, the less partisan, more governmental approach to the Northern Ireland question was being asserted yet again. In July 1989, Peter Brooke replaced Tom King as Northern Ireland Secretary. Brooke caused a stir when he announced on 3 November that the government might talk to Sinn Fein providing that the IRA finally renounced the use of force, arguing that military action could contain, but not defeat, the IRA. He suggested that a 'flexible and imaginative approach' might be needed.[15] The following January, 1990, he began a new series of talks aimed at bringing the parties together, but still with no suspension of the Anglo-Irish Agreement. These talks took place against the background of Brooke's statement in his constituency on 9 November 1990 that Great Britain had no 'strategic or economic interest' in Northern Ireland, and would accept Irish unification if this were by consent.[16] This was in sharp contrast to Tom King's post-Agreement lapse in Brussels when he referred to the permanency of partition, but it still steered some kind of middle course, with the word 'unity' balanced by the word 'consent'. His new round of discussions identified three strands in moves towards a settlement: London–Dublin relations; relations between the north and south of Ireland; and Nationalist–Unionist relations within Northern Ireland. The most difficult of these were North–South relations, which raised a particular problem when a Dublin Court declared in March 1990 that the unification of Ireland embodied in Articles 2 and 3 of the 1937 Irish Constitution were not a mere aspiration, but a 'constitutional imperative'[17] – and this some five years after Dr Garret Fitzgerald had acknowledged the problem that these Articles posed for a move towards peace in the north (while feeling unable to make any move to modify them).[18]

The dual nature of the Irish question in British politics was illustrated in 1992, when the 'government' aspect of the context co-existed with the 'political' character of the question. In January 1992, Peter Brooke shocked the whole of Northern Ireland when he was persuaded to sing on Irish television's 'The Late Late Show', and his attending a rugby match the following day, immediately after the massacre of seven Protestant workmen in Co. Tyrone. Brooke offered to resign, and normally such a deeply offensive error, and, more importantly, an offer by a Cabinet Minister to resign, would have been seized upon by the Opposition in Parliament. But the House of Commons showed its solidarity yet again by fully supporting Brooke in staying at his post.[19] Then, a month later, the politics of Ireland revived, with Kinnock's talks with Molyneux and Paisley explaining in more detail what Labour meant by its Northern Ireland policy statements, and with the Ulster Unionists still hoping for some advantage from a hung parliament. Thus dualism continued after the Conservatives won the general election but with a reduced majority of 21 seats, and the Ulster Unionists, while not of course holding a balance, might yet hope for something from the new parliament, especially as Conservative rifts over the United Kingdom's future in the European Union were soon to be revealed. Meanwhile, following the election, Sir Patrick Mayhew replaced Brooke as Northern Ireland Secretary, and the political talks between the Northern Ireland parties were resumed. The parties remained deadlocked on internal devolution proposals, but the two Unionist parties agreed to talk to Dublin politicians about strand 2 (North–South relations). This, though it seemed to be a small concession, showed that the Unionists were now resolved to end their political exile. But, as always, the difficulty lay in the differing perceptions of what North–South relations and cooperation entailed, with Unionists fearing that matters might slip entirely from their control, and return them to the helplessness they experienced in 1985. The talks continued throughout September and October 1992, but finally ended in November. The problem was that the chief parties concerned were moving at different speeds and in different directions: the Ulster Unionists accepted power-sharing and an 'Inter-Irish Relations Committee' formally linking members of a Northern Ireland Assembly and the Dáil; the SDLP were looking towards a grand, European Union-centred six-man executive commission, with a Northern Ireland Assembly only acting in an advisory capacity. The issue of joint authority over Northern Ireland, shared between London and Dublin, was thus raised again: power-sharing and an Irish dimension, acceptable in 1974, were no longer enough.[20] With the failure of the talks, the Unionists now turned their attention to Westminster, and 'politics', it seemed, replaced 'government' again.

Since the Anglo-Irish Agreement the Ulster Unionists and the Democratic Unionists had, as the Ulster Unionist MP Harold McCusker put it in a dramatic speech in the House of Commons, suffered what they regarded as a betrayal of trust: the Union, the bedrock of their constitutional policy, was now redefined in a way that made their people 'Irish-British hybrids'.[21] But since 1985 they had come once more to the conclusion that the Westminster political game was not yet played out. The Conservative victory in April 1992 was a narrow one; John Major was a new leader, with no Anglo-Irish past to live down; the 'Jezebel' Mrs Thatcher had (it could plausibly be argued) suffered an appropriate fate for her betrayal. Major seemed a reasonably enthusiastic supporter of the Union, in the broadest sense. There were still ominous phrases coming from the Northern Ireland Office, with Sir Patrick Mayhew, the Northern Ireland Secretary, suggesting in December 1992 that Britain was 'neutral' on the issue of Northern Ireland's future place in the United Kingdom; though qualifying this the following March in Bangor, Co. Down, when he assured the people of Northern Ireland that its status could only be altered in response to the will of the majority of the people, and that the government was not neutral in its resolve to 'deliver the people of Northern Ireland from terrorist violence'.[22]

The Ulster Unionists now began to test the ground in the new parliament. The political issue that soon came to dominate British political life was the question of the United Kingdom's relationship with the European Union, and, in particular, the Maastricht Treaty, which a significant group of Conservatives saw as fundamentally undermining the sovereignty of the British parliament. The Ulster Unionists flexed their muscles, voting with Labour against the Maastricht Treaty in November 1992, and following this up with another warning shot in March 1993, when six Ulster Unionists voted with Labour and two abstained; the three Democratic Unionists voted against Maastricht. It seemed that John Major had learned his lesson, for in July 1993 the Ulster Unionists supported the government in another vote on Maastricht, declaring that the Prime Minister had placed himself 'in the forefront of the fight for the Union'.[23] The Ulster Unionist leader, James Molyneux, was a highly respected figure in Westminster, and appeared to have struck up a good understanding with the Prime Minister. Ulster Unionists now reminded themselves that they were the fourth largest party in the House of Commons, and one capable of exercising some influence. They were working their way towards their long-standing demand for a Select Committee on Northern Ireland at Westminster, which Sir Patrick Mayhew had referred to in a speech at the Institute of Irish Studies in Liverpool on 23 April 1993.[24]

Unionists certainly overestimated the political dimension of the British involvement with Northern Ireland. While no British party could be unmindful of the importance of the votes of Northern Irish MPs in a closely contested parliament, it was significant that there never emerged in the Conservative Party a group of pro-Unionist members who might aspire to threaten their own front bench over Northern Ireland as they were doing over British membership of the European Union. MPs might be prepared even to forfeit the party whip over their opposition to a deeper commitment to Europe, but they were not inclined to push matters so far over Ireland; nor could Ireland act as a kind of fault-finder, revealing deeper pro and anti-Thatcherite sentiments in the party at large. Labour were of course glad of any support in embarassing the government over Europe; but when the Unionists voted for the government, some Labour MPs spoke in terms that suggested they thought Unionist votes ought not to have the same weight as those of other parties: an extraordinary view of the working of parliamentary democracy, but one that showed how limited the Unionist choices were, particularly so long as their most committed parliamentary foe, Kevin MacNamara, was Labour's shadow Northern Secretary (Macnamara had on one occasion expressed his concern lest reforms in Northern Ireland might serve to weaken Nationalist sentiment there, and in so doing strengthen the Union).[25]

II

Politics and Government: but there was a third strand to British political involvement in Ireland, that can also be traced back to earlier times, that of clandestine approaches and secret contacts with the more extreme elements in Irish Nationalist politics. In Gladstone's day, this meant finding out Charles Stewart Parnell's political mind through the intermediary of Mrs Katharine O'Shea; for although Parnell was fundamentally a rather conservative Nationalist, his tactics in placing himself at the head of the Land League, his defiant speeches, and his willingness to establish links with the Fenian Brotherhood, made him appear extreme in the eyes of British public opinion. In Lloyd George's time, contacts were maintained with Sinn Fein even at the height of the Black and Tan war, some of which reached almost farcical proportions, such as the time when Lord Derby made a secret visit to Dublin under the pseudonym of 'Mr Edwards'. Harold Wilson in the 1970s entered into discussions with the IRA. It might be argued that such contacts were a necessary part of an anti-terrorist campaign in which there was little likelihood of victory for either the state or its enemies; but in the first couple of years of John Major's premiership it appeared unlikely that there could be any common ground on which Republican and Government envoys could meet. The IRA stepped up its offensive in Great Britain, making terrorist attacks on British cities, including a bomb in the Baltic Exchange in the City of London on 10 April 1992 that caused £800 million worth of damage, and seemed to throw the financial capital into despair. New security measures were introduced hurriedly, but there was the feeling that the bomber could always get through: hardly surprising when, just over a year earlier, No. 10 Downing Street had been the object of a mortar attack which only narrowly missed its target.[26] Inevitably there was loss of life; on 20 March 1993 a three-year-old boy was killed, and 56 people injured, in an IRA bomb attack in Warrington; a few days later a 12-year-old boy died of injuries sustained in the explosion.[27] This event provoked a deep and widespread condemnation of the IRA terrorist campaign, though it is true to say that this event was greeted with a lesser sense of outrage in Northern Ireland, where such deaths were hardly new or surprising.

But at the same time, other hints and signals were being thrown out by the Government. In December 1992, Sir Patrick Mayhew indicated that troops could be withdrawn from the streets of Northern Ireland and Sinn Fein included in talks about the future of the province if the IRA ended its campaign. In April 1993, in the aftermath of the Warrington outrage, the Prime Minister referred to the need to 'catch the mood, to achieve a political accommodation'.[28] By March 1993 the government was already involved in secret talks with Martin McGuinness, a leading Sinn Fein spokesman, and former member of the IRA, an organisation to whose membership he once professed himself proud to belong.[29] These talks were important because they coincided with the beginning of a new set of talks between the leader of constitutional nationalism in Northern Ireland, John Hume, and the president of Provisional Sinn Fein, Gerry Adams. The two had first met in January 1988 to discuss whether or not they could find common ground on a settlement; and these preliminary discussions were influenced by the British intimation that, as Hume put it, 'Britain is now saying that she has no interest of her own in being here and that her only interest is to see agreement among the people who share the island of Ireland'.[30] The renewed secret dialogue between Hume and Adams was revealed on 10–11 April 1993, and, again, Hume stressed the importance of the language now being used by British political figures, in particular Peter Brooke's statement in November 1990 that Great Britain had no 'selfish strategic or economic' interest in Northern Ireland.[31] But Sinn Fein was also feeling the strain of maintaining its dual role as revolutionary Republican party and seeker after a popular electoral mandate that would vindicate its claim that its strength rested on the democratic will of the people. In Republican rhetoric the 'people' consisted of the 'true' will of the nation as discerned and made flesh by Republicans; but not the awkward tendency of the real people to behave in ways other than that dictated by the revolutionary will of the mythic Irish nation. Gerry Adams tried to reconcile these opposites when he declared that the Anglo-Irish Agreement, which affirmed the right of the majority to remain in the United Kingdom, was a flawed document, but that it also showed that the British could be moved in the right direction by Republican pressure.[32]

However, it was also the case that Republicanism could be 'moved in the right direction' by British pressure. In October 1988 the British government announced that it was placing a ban on the broadcasting of direct statements by representatives of Sinn Fein, which was only partly sidestepped by the media's expedient of employing actors to read out the banned statements and speeches.[33] The Brooke–Mayhew talks, though they ended in failure, pointedly excluded Sinn Fein. There was a real danger that Sinn Fein's support, established as it was in a heartland in West Belfast that was plagued by chronic economic and social problems, might come to be seen as a mere manifestation of this deprived context, rather than the autonomous ideology of a dedicated part of the nation. Adams now sought to construct what he called a 'broader, deeper, sustainable political consensus' which should be based on the unity of nationalists both north and south.[34] And while it is hard to believe that Provisional Sinn Fein's vice-president, Martin McGuinness, would ever have sent a message to the British government using the words 'the conflict is over but we need your advice on how to bring it to a close' (which he is alleged by the British to have communicated to them on 22 February 1993),[35] the significance of the exchanges must be seen as part of the wider nationalist dialogue that Hume and Adams now admitted: one in which, they declared, they accepted that the most pressing question facing the people of Britain and

Ireland was 'the question of lasting peace'. They chose their words carefully:

> In striving for that end, we accept that an internal settlement is not a solution because it obviously does not deal with all the relationships at the heart of the problem. We accept that the Irish people as a whole have a right to national self-determination. This is a view shared by a majority of the people of the island, though not by all its people. The exercise of self-determination is a matter for agreement between the people of Ireland. It is the search for that agreement and the means of achieving it on which we will be concentrating.[36]

Secret contacts between Sinn Fein and the British government continued, but it was clear that the two differed about what was meant by an 'agreed solution', with Sinn Fein demanding that there must be an end to the British upholding of the 'Unionist veto' on ending partition, and the British insisting that it could not make an 'imposed settlement'.[37] Meanwhile, the IRA campaign picked up momentum again, with the bombing of the centre of Belfast and other urban centres in Northern Ireland. In September 1993, Hume and Adams issued their second statement which declared their intention to involve the British and Irish governments in the consideration of their broad principles of agreement. On 27 September the Loyalist Ulster Defence Association declared that it was time for all Unionists to put themselves in a state of readiness 'in defence of their religious and political beliefs' in the face of the 'final act of betrayal'. The UVF now stepped up its campaign against the Catholic people, claiming that it was justified in assassinating 'nationalists'.[38] The spiral of violence culminated in the IRA bombing of a fish shop on the Protestant Shankill Road on 23 October as part of their desire to hunt down prominent loyalists; they succeeded in murdering nine innocent civilians, including women and children. A week later the UVF retaliated with a machine gun attack on a public house in Greysteel Co. Londonderry; seven people were killed and another died later.

It was now that the British government showed that it had learned much from its hard experience of its involvement in Northern Ireland in the past decade. The 1970s were a period when British politicians were obliged to cope with what was for their generation a wholly novel problem: a conflict of nationality in the United Kingdom, which was supposed to have been left behind some time in the 1920s. This led them into many blunders, culminating in their disastrous handling of the IRA hunger strike in 1981 which only facilitated the electoral rise of Sinn Fein, and a widespread wave of sympathy for the hunger strikers both in Ireland and abroad. The Anglo-Irish Agreement was a bold stroke, and one which undoubtedly gained much support for the British government internationally; and, although it had failed to live up to expectations, it showed that the British involvement of Dublin in the Northern Ireland predicament could offer political dividends, particularly in discomfiting Sinn Fein and lending support to the constitutional nationalists, even if the price was the alienation of the Ulster Protestants. The danger now was that the rather directionless style of British policy after the failure of the Brooke–Mayhew talks would leave a vacuum which the Hume–Adams dialogue might fill; and the Irish government, for its part, appeared to want to distance itself from the Hume–Adams position following the Shankill bombing.[39] It might be opportune to mobilize the London–Dublin axis once again, and on 29 October the British and Irish prime ministers, John Major and Albert Reynolds, issued a joint statement. This reiterated the point that there must be support from the majority of people living in Northern Ireland for constitutional change; that change could not be achieved by violence; and that the renunciation of violence would result in an imaginative response from the two governments.[40] The Hume–Adams initiative must give way to joint action by the British and Irish governments. Early in November, John Major had declared that it would 'turn his stomach' to talk to Adams and his like;[41] but on 18 November the secret talks between the British government and Irish Republicans were exposed by Martin McGuinness, probably in response to John Major's speech at the Guildhall on 15 November in which he said that there could be 'no secret deals, no rewards for terrorists'.[42] The revelation that if there had been no secret deals, then at least there had been secret talks, may have provoked an embarrassed British government into pressing on with what now appeared to be a real opportunity to seize the initiative; but the government was also increasingly certain that the Republican front was not solid, and that there were those in its ranks who wanted to move towards a political settlement[43] (though one in which the military power of the IRA could still play a part, if at one remove). The Irish government was in a receptive mood, and needed a policy success for its own ends. The path to a joint policy statement was not smooth. On 3 December at a meeting in Dublin, Major and Reynolds failed to agree on a declaration;[44] but on 15 December, at Downing Street, they managed to issue a joint statement that became the 'Downing Street Declaration'.

III

The Downing Street Declaration was, in retrospect, a major breakthrough for British policy in Ireland, and it was made at a time when the Conservative government and the Ulster Unionists were still, apparently, in a mutually beneficial relationship; on 16 December the Leader of the House of Commons, Tony Newton, stated that 'the government have decided to embark on consultations with other parties on the basis that the time for a Northern Ireland Select Committee has now come'.[45] This was a long-standing desire of both the Democratic and the Ulster Unionists, and, not surprisingly, there was much Labour disgust at what they saw as 'collusion'; and although a formal deal of the Committee in return for Unionist support of the government on Maastricht in July 1993 was later denied, it is clear that Major and James Molyneux managed to communicate through the means of silence.[46] Here, then, were contradictory signals, for the Declaration suggested strongly that the British government was willing enough to end the Union if most people in Northern Ireland so desired. The British government reiterated its claim that it had no 'selfish, strategic or economic interest in Northern Ireland'. This was balanced by the concession that Northern Ireland's 'statutory constitutional guarantee' was reaffirmed by both Dublin and London. Then the Declaration upheld the 'democratic wish of the greater number of the people of Northern Ireland on the issue of whether they prefer to support the Union or a sovereign united Ireland'. If the day came when a united Ireland was desired, then both governments reaffirmed:

> a binding obligation that they will, for their part, introduce the necessary legislation to give effect to this, or equally to any measure of agreement on future relationships in Ireland which the people living in Ireland may themselves freely so determine without external impediment.

The Irish government acknowledged that 'it would be wrong to attempt to impose a united Ireland in the absence of the freely given consent of a majority of the people of Northern Ireland'. The civil rights of both communities must be guaranteed and safeguarded, and Dublin promised to review any 'obstacles' that offended Unionists; Articles 2 and 3 of the Irish Constitution were specifically mentioned, and the Irish Government was willing to 'put forward and support' proposals for change. But a permanent end to violence was a prerequisite for any moves towards a settlement; and dialogue would be confined to 'demo-cratically mandated parties which establish a commitment to exclusively peaceful methods'. The Irish government pro-posed the establishment of a 'Forum for Peace and Reconcilia-tion' to make recommendations, and both governments appealed to 'all concerned to grasp the opportunity for a new departure'.[47]

But if the Declaration was, in retrospect, a highly significant document, it hardly seemed so at the time. The initiative was designed primarily to bring Sinn Fein into the world of politics, out from its twilight semi-revolutionary exile. This, at first, it signally failed to do; and Sinn Fein's delaying tactics, demanding 'clarification' of certain parts of the text, while all the time seeking desperately to avoid clarification lest this compromise their Republican credentials, exposed the British government to the danger that Sinn Fein would engage the government in its own, chosen dialogue, and win more concessions before violence stopped – if indeed it were going to stop. The IRA, for its part, kept up the pressure, but again sought to place the British at a disadvantage through declaring a 72-hour ceasefire to come into effect on 5 April 1994, giving the government the opportunity to 'overcome its difficulties'.[48] But the British government found that the Declaration, while it had its gains and its losses in these developments, was gradually giving it the edge in its dealings with Sinn Fein. The involvement of the Dublin government made it hard for Sinn Fein to repudiate what was, after all, a promise that it could be an equal partner in the proposed 'Forum for Peace and Reconciliation'. In January 1994, Albert Reynolds removed the long-standing broadcasting ban on Sinn Fein and suggested that a settlement would result in an amnesty for those convicted of terrorist acts.[49] The brief nature of the IRA ceasefire of 5 April, and Sinn Fein's adamant stand against the Declaration in its conference at Letterkenny in July were greeted with a hostile and disbelieving response, not only in Britain, but in Ireland as well. America now began to play an increasingly important role. In February 1994 the United States gave Gerry Adams a visa to enter the country to address the American Committee on Foreign Policy, despite British objections; but the price of American benevolence was that Adams must think again, and seriously, about committing himself and Sinn Fein to wholly democratic ways.[50] For Sinn Fein to stem this tide, which was in some respects at least running in its favour, and for the IRA to continue its campaign unabated, would deprive the Republican movement as a whole of any hope of exercising whatever political influence it could muster for a very long time to come. On 31 August 1994 the IRA declared a ceasefire in terms which suggested that this was not a mere propaganda ploy, but the result of a serious reassessment of its whole military strategy.[51]

The British government could feel some satisfaction at this outcome, and take much of the credit for it; it had called Sinn Fein's bluff, and asked the Republican movement to make good its claim that it had a democratic mandate for its cause. But the price of this success was that the peace movement had broadened out, incorporating not only the Republic of Ireland, but also the United States of America and even, morally at least, the European Union; and this must make it hard for the British to retain full control of any settlement proposals. The fact that the Downing Street Declaration was a joint one with Ireland meant of course that any further progress must be made with the consent of the Irish as well as the British governments; this had provoked difficulties in the past, as the Irish perspective was different from that of a British government which was more cautious, not only because of the long terrorist onslaught that its citizens had endured, in Great Britain as well as Northern Ireland, but because John Major's government must be careful not to alienate the Unionists. This need was not merely political, though Major still found Unionist votes important in parliament; Major had yet to convince the Loyalist paramilitary organisations that they were not to be betrayed, and on a visit to Belfast on 16 September he promised a referendum on the outcome of the talks process, and no 'secret deals'.[52] On 10 October the Combined Loyalist Military Command announced a ceasefire; its spokesman explained that 'The Prime Minister had given undertakings – firm undertakings – that Ulster's position within the United Kingdom would be safe'.[53]

The British government reacted to the IRA ceasefire with caution. On 4 September, John Major spoke on television of the need for a 'copper-bottomed' guarantee from the IRA that the ceasefire was permanent; but the broadcasting ban on Sinn Fein was removed on 16 September. When Albert Reynolds greeted Gerry Adams in Dublin on 6 September the British government warned that this was premature; on the same day John Major met the Reverend Ian Paisley in Downing Street and ordered him to leave the room when he refused to say that he accepted Major's word that there had been no secret deals with the IRA before the ceasefire announcement.[54] The Ulster Unionist leader, James Molyneux, met no such ignominious fate; but the weakness of Unionism in the face of the British government's desire to build on the joint loyalist/IRA ceasefires was soon to be revealed, when on 1 February 1995 *The Times* newspaper printed details of what it claimed was the long-awaited British and Irish document setting out their views on a framework for peace and a permanent settlement to secure peace. The leaked proposals referred to a 'joint North–South Irish authority with radical executive powers'; 'harmonisation' of agricultural, trade, education and health policies; a 'new cross-border institution', involving members of the Irish parliament; and a devolved Northern Ireland Assembly which would bring together senior civil servants and politicians. 'Membership', the leak revealed, 'will be compulsory for the relevant heads of department in each administration'; and *The Times* went on to claim that 'the executive powers would be sweeping', with the joint body having policy-making powers 'for the whole island in respect of the challenges and opportunities of the European Union'. It stated that the government had not yet completed its proposals, that there was no question of joint authority and that anything that was finally agreed would be subject to a referendum; but in a leader *The Times* warned that, although 'strictly speaking' this was not joint authority, the proposals would give the Republic of Ireland a wide range of executive responsibilities over the affairs of the North, and encourage it to demand more: 'A road has been marked out which leads – if it leads anywhere – to joint authority and eventual unification'.[55]

This report was greeted by Unionists with shock and disbelief. The Ulster Unionist, John Taylor, a man of acknowledged moderate opinions and a broader view than most of his colleagues, stated that 'if the report is correct, then Downing Street is betraying the British majority community in Northern Ireland'.[56] John Major and his Cabinet did not deny the essential authenticity of the document; but he responded rapidly by making a television broadcast the following day in which he insisted that it was wrong to see the document as a blueprint for a united Ireland which would be imposed on the North. In the House of Commons, Sir Patrick Mayhew said that the leak was 'a few phrases lifted highly selectively from a lengthy negotiating text employed in the discussions with the Irish Government but upon which the governments have not agreed'. There would, in any case, be the 'triple lock' of parties, people and parliament against any imposed settlement.[57] The crisis atmosphere at Westminster was very real; television and radio reporters spoke of 'despair' that the whole process was about to founder, and Northern Ireland and Britain would be plunged back to the dark days of 1985 and 1974, when Unionism declared its refusal to countenance the most radical policy decisions of the British government. The Unionists began to threaten to use their votes in the House to precipitate a general election.[58]

But it was a measure of the determination of the Conservative government, and of the other major British parties, not to let this Northern Ireland question place politics over the arts of government, that they all agreed that the peace process must not be jeopardised. The British and Irish governments urged their civil servants to prepare for an early release of the Framework document, and on 22 February John Major and the Irish prime minister John Bruton stood shoulder to shoulder at Hillsborough Castle, County Down, to demonstrate that they were agreed about the future of the process. Major appealed to Unionists; Bruton spoke more for nationalists. The document proposed a Northern Ireland Assembly elected by proportional representation with wide-ranging legislative powers; a North–South body of elected representatives of the Assembly and the Irish Parliament; the introduction and support by the Irish Government for 'changes in the Irish Constitution, so that no territorial claim of right to jurisdiction over Northern Ireland contrary to the wish of a majority of its people is asserted'; a parliamentary forum of representatives from the North and South to hold wider discussions; changes in British law to recognise the right of the people of Northern Ireland to decide their future; a referendum in both the North and the South, with a majority needed in both to approve any settlement plan. The governments of Dublin and London committed themselves to protect the civil, social and cultural rights of all groups in Northern Ireland, and to working closely together for a settlement.[59] The document was framed to offer comfort to all sides in the conflict, and, again, cast the British government (and of course the Irish government as well) in the role of neutral facilitator of a peaceful resolution of the conflict. Unionists criticised the document as a blueprint for an All-Ireland; but there was no more talk of bringing down the Conservative government, no encouragement by the Opposition parties for them to do so, and the same solidarity prevailed in Great Britain over the Framework Document as had done over the Anglo-Irish Agreement and the Power-sharing executive of 1974.

IV

The fact that consensus and bipartisanship was maintained, that public opinion was 'neutral', and that the Ulster Unionist has no option but to make the best of a rather unfavourable situation, all requires some consideration. The Labour Party had always declared its support for a united Ireland 'by consent', though this did not prevent Labour spokesmen from suggesting in the lean years of the 1980s that Labour might meet Unionist calls for a change in the way Northern Ireland legislation was dealt with at Westminster; and the strident call for Irish unity was now more muted, with the emphasis placed on discussion in Northern Ireland itself on constitutional change.[60] But now the Labour party placed itself in the middle, with its new leader, Tony Blair, announcing at its October 1995 Conference that he would not play politics with people's lives in Northern Ireland. The Liberal Democrats always saw themselves as leaning more towards honest brokerage than party political values. The Conservatives contained in their ranks some strong supporters of the Union, and when in Opposition in the 1970s came close to accepting the integrationist argument.[61] But Mrs Thatcher had set the tone with her acknowledgement that 'Ireland was different', and that there must be some special approach to this aspect of the defence of the United Kingdom.[62] Conservative MPs and Constituency parties would not jeopardise party unity over Ulster as they did over Britain's future in the European Union; and, even if they were tempted to do so, they could not play upon genuine Conservative fears, as could the Eurosceptics; the game was not worth the candle. John Major followed the Thatcherite line on the Union, in that he insisted that Scottish and Welsh devolution would jeopardise its future, but that Northern Ireland devolution was, on the other hand, essential for the security of the Kingdom: a means not of weakening, but of strengthening it.[63] This was not new; proposals for 'Home Rule all round' had emerged parallel with the Irish Question between 1912 and 1921; but they always foundered on the assumption that what was good for Ireland was not necessarily good for the Kingdom as a whole. The weakness of the Ulster Unionist position was revealed in a survey of constituency opinion in 1989, when 48 out of 51 constituencies (96 per

153

cent) rated Northern Ireland as 'very' or 'fairly' important, but did not draw the conclusion that this assessment merited an integrationalist policy.[64]

The parties' ability to maintain their consensus approach to the Northern Ireland problem was reinforced by the failure of British public opinion (probably caused by the desire of the political elite to exclude the region from political party controversy) to formulate any coherent mind on the subject. While it remained the case that there was always a disposition to 'bring the troops home', which Republicans were anxious to exploit, there remained a determination to maintain a firm stand against individual IRA attacks in Great Britain. It was often felt that the cost of staying in Northern Ireland was disproportionate to the gains for Britain. When it came to answering questions about the region's future, a *Daily Express-Mori* poll in 1987 showed that 22 per cent were in favour of immediate withdrawal; 34 per cent were in favour of keeping the troops there for as long as was necessary; and 39 per cent called for a phased withdrawal. But on the question of a political settlement, 58 per cent favoured a solution at odds with the republican call for Irish unity: 29 per cent were in favour of Northern Ireland remaining part of the United Kingdom; 29 per cent supported an independent Northern Ireland state (which, while it would damage everyone, would certainly end in a defeat for Republicans); and only 27 per cent supported Irish unity.[65] There was also the question (which opinion polls raise rather than resolve) of how the public would want the details of policy to be worked out. A lack of enthusiasm for retaining Northern Ireland within the United Kingdom might not amount to supporting the expulsion of a region from the state against its will. And of course these ambiguities about one region in the Kingdom might raise problems about other nations; especially Scotland, which in the 1980s and early 1990s grew increasingly restive under Conservative rule, and was promised a devolved parliament by the Labour Party. It is doubtful whether the English people knew or cared anything more about Scotland or Wales than they did about Northern Ireland. Calls for the 'British people' to have an overriding veto on what the people of Northern Ireland wanted was at odds with the acceptance in

British politics that the nations/regions had in some way, at times ill-defined, the right to have their views heard and acted upon. Scotland had its own political culture, which, while it was not as distinct from England's as that of Northern Ireland, was nonetheless a dangerous one to ignore or misunderstand. Opinion Polls and the media produced instant reactions to the unfolding of events in Northern Ireland, but the general impression they gave over an extended period was that of incoherence and mystification, interspersed with outbursts of irritation at the unreasonable behaviour of all parties in Northern Ireland. There was a vague feeling that Irish unity in some shape or form would be, to use the celebrated cliché 'a good thing'; but there was also an acceptance that the people of Northern Ireland should be allowed to decide their own future. These sentiments could be said to sit easily beside the government's speeches, declarations and documents since the Anglo-Irish Agreement: a sympathy towards Irish unity aspirations, a neutral stance on the future of Northern Ireland, but no attempt at compulsory expulsion of the region from the United Kingdom.

This was the domestic context in which the search for a settlement following the ceasefires and the framework document would be set. But the Northern Ireland Question had also assumed a more internationalist character. This, again, was not completely new; in 1919–21, Lloyd George was influenced by the views of British Imperial statesmen such as Jan Smuts of South Africa; in the 1930s the British government again found itself under pressure from Dominions' premiers not to take too strong a line when Eamon de Valera launched his economic war and his assault upon the terms of the 1921 treaty settlement.[66] Now the European Union, and, more importantly, the United States of America stood firmly behind the peace process. In March 1995 President Clinton met Gerry Adams, and conferred a significant tincture of respectability upon the Sinn Fein President.[67] This did not mean that the British and Irish governments were in any way deprived of their primary role in the process; but it emphasised again that this was not 'the Irish Question in British politics' purely and simply, but was a matter of international actors, including the Irish and British states, steering the process through to a conclusion.

A final settlement, if it is possible, is still a distant prospect, and may yet be jeopardised by an IRA refusal to move towards 'decommissioning' arms. But the past 25 years, and especially the last decade, have revealed the British concept of the broad outlines of a settlement: some form of power-sharing in a devolved government; an 'Irish Dimension', including cross-bor-der institutions, however defined; and a studied, and by now routine, insistence that, in the conflict of nationality in Northern Ireland, the British state stands resolutely neutral: the flirtation with integration of the late 1970s was ephemeral. Party politics may marginally influence the way in which these concepts are realised; but not even the most desperate needs of a Conservative administration, nor of a Labour party and Liberal-Democratic party in the wilderness of prolonged Opposition, can shake the fundamental desire of the British parties and public opinion to play the role of facilitator and 'honest broker'. This was seen as early as 1972, in the second reading of the Bill which introduced direct rule over Northern Ireland, when the Conservative govern-ment of Edward Heath counted 483 votes against only 18.[68] Unfortunately, the people, parties and organisations in the North are anxious to ascertain on whose side (if any) the British are honestly neutral: neutrality is an unfamiliar term of discourse in Northern Ireland politics. But, whatever the flaws in British policy over the last decade, and however fortuitous its successes appear to be, it has at least obliged Northern Irish politicians, constitutional and Sinn Fein, nationalist and Unionist, to take stock of and reconsider their position.[69]

CONCLUSION

A QUESTION FOR BRITAIN

A study of the Irish Question in British politics offers a kind of commentary on, and illustration of, the character of the British political tradition itself; indeed, it might be said, without undue cynicism, to throw more light on British than on Irish history. In the nineteenth century Britain was a Protestant nation and a great power; in the course of the present century she was transformed into a secular country and one increasingly preoccupied with distracting concepts like 'decline' and 'economic dislocation'. From the 1860s onwards she was made aware of regional and even national distinctions within her constitution; but from 1923 Britain saw herself as a homogeneous community, not all that different in national character perhaps from Shakespeare's England (and, like John of Gaunt, happily able to equate 'England', the 'sceptr'd isle', with the whole of Britain).

This has not always been appreciated by Irish political parties, particularly Ulster Unionists, who have hardly moved their conception of what 'England' is beyond the first decades of the twentieth century. Thus the strategic, religious and nationalist preoccupations of British politicians and indeed the British public between 1868 and 1914 enabled the Irish Question to obtain a lodgement in the centre of British politics, and allowed Irish political groups to exercise a considerable influence on the perceptions and tactics of the major British parties. The special circumstances of the party system at Westminster between 1906 and 1914 placed the Irish Question in a crucial relationship to the goals and strategies of the British Unionist and Liberal Parties; but once these circumstances altered, as they did after 1915, then the Irish Question was placed in a different context, and its diagnosis and treatment was shaped, and made possible, by the new postwar political world: a world that after 1923 became obsessed with the politics of economics in which the Irish Question could find no ready identification.

This was not only a question of mood or atmosphere; for in politics organisation is all important, and after 1918 the British party political system altered profoundly, with the withdrawal of the Irish Nationalist MPs from Westminster, and the reduction after 1921 of the Northern Irish contingent there to only twelve seats. This made the House of Commons a more insular – but, it must be said, less controversial – political arena, conforming once more to Walter Bagehot's classic description of it as an institution where, though the atoms were hot, the body politic was cool. The establishment of two political capitals in Belfast and Dublin accelerated this process, for now Irish political groups had their own local stage on which to act their parts. This did not prevent Nationalist obsession with London while de Valera was Taoiseach; but it prevented any major incursion of the Irish Question into British politics, especially since the Ulster Unionists at Westminster had few opportunities and no desire to exploit the party battle there in their own interest. The advisability of this low-level strategy was highlighted by its temporary absence in 1965 when the Labour government's anger was aroused by what it almost seemed to regard as the illegitimate parliamentary votes of the Ulster Unionist MPs – and unwelcome attention was drawn to the place of Northern Ireland in the United Kingdom which helped bring hostile criticism down on the Unionist Party's heads.

As well as political circumstances, British political culture was important in shaping and reshaping the role of the Irish Question in British politics. It cannot be said that Ireland was often at the centre of British political attention immediately after the Union of 1800; and no new political structures were created to accommodate this alteration in the constitution of the United Kingdom. Yet the British political elite was more aware of Ireland in the nineteenth century than is its counterpart of the twentieth. Partly this was because of the Irish political presence at Westminster, which enabled Irish affairs to work their way into the straitjacket of British party politics: Ireland could serve the parties as much as the parties could serve Ireland. But there does appear to have been a greater willingness to evolve some idea of what Ireland was, and what Ireland needed, however imperfect this might be. After 1921, however, the development of a 'deeply self-centred, self-obsessed metropolitan political culture' in Britain accelerated.[1] This culture was not only ignorant of things Irish; it also had little concept of the edge of the Union in general. It was more comfortable, as well as politically convenient, to reject or smother unwanted intrusions into the world of 'domestic' British politics. The British parliament's convention that it would regard the discussion of matters relating to Northern Ireland as beyond its brief was an example of how persuasive this mood could be. Yet Britain still continued to exert a dominant influence on the development and shape of Irish political controversies, in 1986 as in 1868. For, whether it be regarded as a blessing or a curse, Ireland was, and (according to the dictates of geography) still remains, in very close proximity to Great Britain, to what many Irish people persist in calling the 'mainland'. And so British recognition of an 'Irish Question', her diagnosis of it, the actions she takes according to her lights, is a major, perhaps the major influence on the outcome of Ireland's political destiny. The fact that Ireland was a British question in the nineteenth and twentieth centuries has left both parts of the country with the legacies of British political endeavour, as well as British political conflict. When Gladstone sought to create a conservative, stable, settled Ireland, still attached to the Union, he first picked out the Church of Ireland, then the landlords and then the Union itself (or, more precisely, the Union as it stood unmodified by a measure of Home Rule for Ireland), as the issue to be tackled. Whether the Church or the landlords merited this unwelcome attention, whether or not Home Rule was a workable compromise, is not here in question; but the definition of these issues provided the agenda for a whole generation of British politicians, and the measures they took, ecclesiastical, agrarian or administrative, largely shaped the making of modern Ireland. Similarly, the British decision to recognise and give self-government to the two main groups in Ireland in 1920, the Irish Nationalists and Ulster Unionists, had important consequences for the minorities left behind in the north and south. Neville Chamberlain's decision to cede control of the treaty ports to de Valera in 1938 enabled Ireland to remain neutral in World War II, and allowed Northern Ireland to claim some goodwill from Britain in 1949. And the British recognition that Northern Ireland must be 'reformed', their pressure on the Unionist Party, their search after 1972 for a political arrangement in Northern Ireland which might win the allegiance of the main political groupings and identities there, has shaped, and will shape, the future of the province. And while Britain is not the 'honest broker' that she likes to think she is, the British presence at least imposes a framework − however shaky and unsatisfactory − in which relations between majority and minority might be adjusted through a political, instead of a bloody and revolutionary process, from which militant Unionism would emerge triumphant.

It might be asked in what sense Ireland can or should still be a Question for British politics, when British politics has so little to gain and so much to lose in Ireland. But withdrawal from Northern Ireland, while it is spoken of and indeed approved of by large sections of British public opinion, would pose problems for Britain, the humiliation of the British government, the creation of a world 'trouble spot' dangerously near to the mainland. It is less damaging for Britain to keep her Irish Question, at least for the foreseeable future. Geography and politics created the Question in the first place; and geography and politics after all constitute two of the eternal verities of the Anglo-Irish connection.

The relationship between the Irish Question and British politics can be summed up simply enough, without doing violence to the complexities. English, or British, ministers sought to reconcile Ireland to the Union by effecting social, economic and political changes which, as Disraeli put it, 'a revolution would effect by force'. But the British public had to be convinced of the necessity and efficacy of these policies; and for it to devote too much time to Irish affairs was, as even Gladstone admitted, 'against nature'. Ireland was, and some of it still is, governed by British rather than (in this case) Northern Irish public opinion; and, as Charles Greville put it in 1844, much difference of opinion prevails 'as to . . . what the people of England could be brought to consent, and what the people of Ireland would be content to receive'. This difference in perception constituted the Irish Question from Gladstone onwards, and underlay the various Irish bills, acts and legislation that fill the pages of British history. Its widening to dangerous proportions has been, and would be again, a crisis, not only for the north, but for the island of Ireland and the whole British Isles.

That its narrowing comprises the next, and most vulnerable, phase of the Irish Question for contemporary British politics is as true in 1996 as it was in 1985. The paradox today is that the Irish state also needs to close this gap, rather than rely on its own traditions when confronting the North. It is thus that it can best contribute to the making of a stable settlement which will help British politics negotiate the complexities in its search for an answer to the (Northern) Irish Question. But, whatever the importance of Irish and American involvement in what has become known as the Peace Process, it is still the case that, as so often in the past, the fate of Ireland hangs ultimately on the decisions of British politicians.

EPILOGUE:

CLINTON IN IRELAND

President Cliton's triumphant, perhaps even triumphal, visit to Northern Ireland and the Irish Republic at the end of November and the beginning of December 1995 seemed to mark a significant development in the Northern Ireland question. The President received what *The Times*' reporter called 'a hero's welcome' as he travelled around the North 'preaching reconciliation and injecting vital momentum into the peace process'. Unionists and Nationalists alike praised the President's visit; and Clinton told those who would use violence that 'You are the past: your day is over'.[1] Moreover, the visit encouraged the British and Irish governments to find a means of resolving (or, perhaps more accurately, concealing) their differences over the question of the de-commissioning of at least some terrorist arms through the so-called twin-track approach, whereby moves towards talks between the political parties in Northern Ireland could take place at the same time as an international commission under the chairmanship of the American Senator George Mitchell would examine, and make recommendations, on this issue. Both preparatory talks on the future of Northern Ireland, and the report of the Commission, would thus be completed in time for all-party negotiations to begin in earnest by the end of February 1996. The Irish Taoiseach, Mr John Bruton, declared that the visit of 'the most powerful politician in the world' would give the people of Northern Ireland and their politicians 'the confidence that they need to make the compromises, to give the ground that is essential if the potential of the twin-track process is to be realised'.[2]

This occasion marked what might be regarded as the high watermark of the internationalisation of the Northern Ireland question. An American President in Ireland was giving the lead to both the British and Irish governments, and to the political parties, in revitalising the peace process. It was not long before the old realities surfaced once again. The Sinn Féin President, Gerry Adams, was less than forthcoming in supporting the de-commissioning body led by Senator Mitchell. The IRA, for its part, made it clear that they were hostile to the whole idea, warning that it was 'ludicrous' to suggest de-commissioning arms either through what it called the 'front' or 'back' door.[3] Adams sought to play down the significance of the IRA statement by declaring that it was 'reiterating and stating the obvious'; the Reverend Ian Paisley for the Democratic Unionists sought to play up its significance by insisting that 'the Clinton bubble, blown up by Bruton and Major, has burst'; the Ulster Unionist deputy leader, John Taylor, warned that the IRA was 'still intransigent, they still want to keep their arms and there is just no change in their situation'. For the SDLP, Dr. Joseph Hendron spoke of his disappointment at the statement, but claimed that 'all is not lost'.[4] Equally important, and perhaps more ominous, was the paramilitary attack upon petty criminals in Roman Catholic areas, resulting in murder and intimidation, which dismayed the British Government; but not to the point that they wished to acknowledge that the cease-fire was crumbling, and might yet drift into a renewal of paramilitary violence on a wider scale. If these attacks were to be directed at members of the Protestant community, then the cease-fire would indeed be in serious jeopardy.

These events took place against a background – or from the purely British point of view – foreground of increasing disarray amongst the Conservative Party. The party remained deeply divided, and the tensions between Left and Right surfaced in the defection of the Conservative MP, Emma Nicholson to the Liberal Democrats on 29 December 1995. This made the support of the nine Ulster Unionist MPs vital to the survival of a government with a working majority of five, and appeared to raise once again the possibility that an Irish political party would play a key role at Westminster, with all the consequences that would flow from Conservative dependence on Unionist votes. Cardinal Cahal Daly, leader of Ireland's Roman Catholics, warned that it would be 'most unfortunate' if the Conservative's shrinking majority at Westminster influenced the search for peace in Ulster, and allowed the peace to suffer 'because of internal political difficulties'.[5]

Certainly it seemed that, on the face of it, a weakening Conservative Government, and a Labour Opposition scenting further turmoil in government ranks, and perhaps even a sudden general election, offered up new and tempting possibilities for Unionists. But this was to overstate the potential for a new lease of life for the Irish Question in British politics. The Ulster Unionists would be cautious about bringing down a party in government whose policy they were familiar with (however much they disliked it, or parts of it) and helping to replace it with one whose statements on Northern Ireland were hardly controversial, but whose sympathies with the idea of the Union were not yet put to the test of power. There was no forthcoming legislation which might provoke the Unionists to withdraw their support. The Ulster Unionists were inclined to take a cautious line, emphasising the 'independence' of their position, and disclaiming any possibility of 'special deals from the Government'.[6] In any event, Major's close contacts with the former Unionist leader, James Molyneux, hardly suggested that, when key policy decisions on Northern Ireland were to be made, they would be substantially altered by perceptions of what might please Unionists most. Nevertheless, Unionists were, as their security spokesman Mr Ken Maginnis put it, likely to 'make the most of it'.[7]

These developments helped put the Clinton visit into perspective. That the President's speeches and actions made a return to violence more difficult was certainly true; but there were those in the IRA who would not let it deter them if they thought that this was necessary. That the Northern Ireland political parties were eased along the road to negotiations was another result of the Clinton visit; but they would not surrender what they regarded as their vital interests, and Sinn Féin was still hardly a model of democratic and constitutional political party. That the British and Irish Governments were encouraged by the visit to seek a reasonable fudge on the arms issue was certain; but their differences remained, and each government had its own political position, and its own political culture, to take note of; and the prospects of a weakening and perhaps even disintegrating Conservative government at Westminster was bound to create unstable conditions from the point of view of Northern Irish political parties. Above all, the British dimension remained vital. The state of the parties at Westminster, the government's need to steer a careful course through the conflicting wishes of the Northern Ireland parties, its need to keep a watchful eye on international, and especially American official opinion: all these made the resolution of the Question as complex and as difficult in 1996 as it had been when Gladstone introduced his first Home Rule bill in 1886. But it seems safe to say that any party political battles at Westminster and in the country would, as far as Ireland is concerned, prove but shadows compared to the heroic days of the first Home Rule bill. When all was said and done, the Whips' calculation of party arithmetic, and the niceties of government majorities, could be no substitute for the ideologies and belief that marked the introduction of the Irish Question into British politics in the Gladstonian age.

Instead of ideology and belief, the British government showed a desire to use the 'black arts' of politics, balancing concession here with firmness there. The Mitchell Report was published on 24 January, and it stated plainly that there was no hope of the IRA starting to decommission weapons before all-party talks took place. But Mitchell offered a way forward: arms decommissioning might take place during all-party talks, providing that the participants agreed to six conditions before being admitted to the talks. These were a commitment to democratic and exclusively peaceful means of resolving political issues; total disarmament of all paramilitary organisations; to agree to verifiable disarmament to the satisfaction of an independent commission; to renounce the use pof force or the threat of force to influence the outcome of negotiations; to agree to abide by the terms of any settlement rerached in all- party talks; and to end 'punishment beatings'. The British government, faced with this report which undermined its policy of demanding decommissioning before talks, balanced this setback with an announcement by the Prime Minister, Mr Major, that there would be elections for a new assembly in Northern Ireland, a suggestion first put forward by the Ulster Unionists some time ago.

This was a neat piece of political maneuvring; and while it is easy to attribute it to Ulster Unionist numbers in a House of Commons with a diminishing government majority, it is more likely to be a product of the Prime Minister's much underrated political skills, and his experience in balancing competing interests – skills honed in the great Conservative controversy over continuing membership of the European Union. The dual approach to the next stage in the peace process provoked strong opposition from Northern Ireland nationalists, with John Hume accusing Major or 'playing politics' with people's lives. The Government's approach would not have fundamentally alienated the constitutional nationalists, would make the dropping of the precondition of decommissioning arms more acceptable to the Ulster Unionists, and could not easily have been ultimately rejected by Sinn Fein. But Major's balancing act was swept aside by the IRA's ending of its ceasefire on 9 February, when it planted a bomb at the Docklands railway station near the Canary Wharf office block tower. Moreover, it left him open to the accusation that his decision to accept the elections option was responsible for the breakdown of the ceasefire, though the preparations for assembling and planting the bomb must have been made weeks earlier, and is attributable more to the internal stresses and strains in the IRA military command, inspired by a desire not to split over the question of peace and war, even if a renewal of violence might prove counter-productive.

The Dublin government, in its initial reaction to the ending of the ceasefire, almost surrendered to the notion that in some sense the British were to blame for the renewed crisis. Its anger and shock at the bombing in London was real and profound. But the British political parties did not break ranks over Northern Ireland, with the partial exception of the marginalised former Northern Ireland shadow secretary, Kevin MacNamara. Tony Blair echoed John Major's condemnation of the IRA, his criticism of Sinn Fein, and his desire to continue the search for peace. Thus the most contentious issue in contemporary British politics would, as far as the British parties were concerned, remain uncontested ground, and the search for a settlement would continue untroubled, at least, by the rage of party.

REFERENCES

INTRODUCTION

1. D. A. Kerr, *Peel, Priests and Politics* (Oxford, 1982), pp. 115–16.
2. J. L. Hammond, *Gladstone and the Irish Nation* (London, 1964 ed.), p. 32.
3. Kerr, op. cit., p. 117.
4. P. M. H. Bell, *Disestablishment in Ireland and Wales* (London, 1969), pp. 40–1.
5. J. C. Beckett, *The Making of Modern Ireland* (London, 1966 ed.), p. 353.
6. *Spectator*, 'The Unionists and Lord Rosebery', 17 March 1894, quoted in Frank O'Gorman, *British Conservatism: Conservative Thought from Burke to Thatcher* (London, 1986), p. 175.
7. The Earl of Selborne to Joseph Chamberlain, 20 December 1909, MS. Selborne 9/177.
8. See Chamberlain's speeches in 1906, J. Amery, *The Life of Joseph Chamberlain*, Vol. 6 (London, 1969), pp. 594–5, 901–7.
9. K. Robbins, *Core and Periphery in Modern British History* (London, 1985), p. 290.
10. *Economist*, 'A Future for Ulster', 23 August 1969.
11. O. MacDonagh, *States of Mind* (London, 1983), p. 56.
12. D. G. Boyce, *Nationalism in Ireland* (London, 1982), pp. 214–17.
13. R. F. Foster, 'Together and Apart: Anglo-Irish Agreements, 1886–1986', *History Today*, Vol. 36 (May, 1986), pp. 6–9.
14. D. C. Sommervell, *The British Empire* (London, 1930), p. 217.
15. For a typical example of this see T. O. Lloyd, *Empire to Welfare State* (Oxford, 1970).
16. As A. T. Q. Stewart puts it 'Paradoxically they [the penal laws] have been more resented by Catholics since their repeal than they seem to have been by Catholics who lived under them', *The Narrow Ground* (London, 1977), p. 103.
17. The phrase is Conor Cruise O'Brien's; see *The Shaping of Modern Ireland* (London, 1960), p. 13.

CHAPTER 1

1. P. M. H. Bell, *Disestablishment in Ireland and Wales* (London, 1969), pp. 75–6.
2. Ibid., p. 23.
3. Michael Bentley, *Politics without Democracy, 1815–1914* (London, 1969), pp. 204–5.
4. M. Hartigan, A. O'Day and R. Quinault, 'Irish terrorism in Britain', in A. O'Day and Y. Alexander (eds), *Ireland's Terrorist Dilemma* (Amsterdam, 1986), pp. 51–7.
5. Boyce, op. cit., p. 186.
6. Bell, op. cit., pp. 60–1.
7. J. C. Beckett, *The Making of Modern Ireland, 1603–1923*, p. 371.
8. W. E. Vaughan, *Landlords and Tenants in Ireland, 1848–1904* (Dublin, 1985).
9. Boyce, op. cit., p. 220.
10. A. O'Day, *Parnell and the First Home Rule Episode* (Dublin, 1986), p. 40.
11. Bentley, op. cit., p. 230.
12. J. Vincent, *Gladstone and Ireland* (London, 1977), p. 203.
13. Ibid., p. 210, fn. 2.
14. E. D. Steele, 'Gladstone, Irish violence and conciliation', in A. Cosgrove and D. McCartney, *Studies in Irish History* (Dublin, 1980), pp. 72–3.
15. P. Bew, *Charles Stewart Parnell* (Dublin, 1980), pp. 72–3.
16. The general election was postponed because administrative changes required by the franchise and redistribution acts of 1884–85 were not yet complete.
17. The 1885 election resulted in the difference between the Conservatives and Liberals exactly equalling the strength of Parnell's following. See Appendix A.
18. Vincent, op. cit., pp. 220–32.
19. *Dublin Daily Express*, 8 November 1877.
20. H. C. G. Matthew (ed.), *The Gladstone Diaries, Vol. XI, 1883–1886* (Oxford, 1990), p. 381.
21. Ibid., pp. 389–90.
22. Ibid., pp. 429–30, 451.
23. Peter Gordon (ed.), *The Red Earl: the Paper of the Fifth Earl Spencer, 1835–1910* (2 vols; Vol. II, Northampton, 1986), pp. 5–6, 83–90.
24. H. C. G. Matthew, *The Gladstone Diaries, Vol. X, 1881–1883* (Oxford, 1990), p. cii.
25. Ibid., p. cliii, and Vol. XI, p. 500.
26. Ibid., Vol. XI, pp. 516–17.
27. Bew, op. cit., p. 69; Gordon, op. cit., p. 103.
28. O'Day, op. cit, Chs 1–3.

29. Gladstone, 'Further Notes and Queries on the Irish Demand', *Contemporary Review*, Vol. LIII (Jan–June 1888), p. 335.
30. R. F. Foster, *Lord Randolph Churchill: a Political Life* (Oxford, 1981), p. 227.
31. P. Marsh, *The Discipline of Popular Government: Lord Salisbury's Domestic Statecraft, 1881–1902* (Sussex, 1978), pp. 73, 90–4.
32. Foster, op. cit., pp. 252–60.
33. For a local example of this see M. Wainwright, *Ireland not Socialism: a Leeds Election* (Leeds, 1970), pp. 16–19.
34. Gladstone, op. cit., p. 335; J. Loughlin, *Gladstone, Home Rule and the Ulster Question* (Dublin, 1986), pp. 132–42.
35. Marsh, op. cit., p. 157.
36. H. C. G. Matthew (ed.), *The Gladstone Diaries, Vol. XI, 1883–1886* (Oxford, 1990), p. 602.
37. Matthew (ed.), *The Gladstone Diaries, Vol. XII, 1887–1891* (Oxford, 1994), pp. 337–8.
38. Matthew (ed.), *The Gladstone Diaries, Vol. XIII, 1892–1896* (Oxford, 1994), pp. 41–2.
39. Matthew (ed.), *The Gladstone Diaries, Vol. XII*, p. 354.
40. Dicey to Viscount Wolmer, 5 Nov. 1891, MS. Selborne 13/95.
41. D. Brooks (ed.), *The Destruction of Lord Rosebery* (London, 1986), pp. 85, 98, 108.
42. A. Gailey, 'Failure and the Making of the New Ireland', in D. G. Boyce (ed.), *The Revolution in Ireland, 1879–1923* (London, 1987).
43. Catherine B. Shannon, 'The Legacy of Arthur Balfour to Twentieth Century Ireland', in Peter Collins (ed.), *Nationalism versus Unionism: Conflict in Ireland, 1885–1921* (Belfast, 1994), pp. 17–33, at p. 32.
44. Alvin Jackson, *The Ulster Party; Irish Unionists in the House of Commons, 1884–1911* (Oxford, 1989), Ch. 4.
45. C. B. Shannon, 'Arthur Balfour and the Irish Question, 1874–1921', Massachussetts Ph.D., 1975, p. 86.
46. C. Townshend, *Political Violence in Ireland* (Oxford, 1983), p. 212.
47. Shannon, op. cit., p. 146.
48. Ibid., p. 155.
49. John Ramsden, *The Age of Balfour and Baldwin* (London, 1978), p. 17.
50. A. O'Day (ed.) *The Edwardian Age: Conflict and Stability* (London, 1979), p. 123.
51. Ramsden, op. cit., p. 20.

CHAPTER 2

1. David Dutton, *Austen Chamberlain: Gentlemen in Politics* (Bolton, 1985), p. 102.

2. H. J. Hanham, *The Nineteenth Century Constitution* (Cambridge, 1969), p. 192.
3. John Ramsden, *Age of Balfour and Baldwin*, p. 32.
4. See Appendix A.
5. Ronan Fanning, 'The Irish policy of Asquith's government and the cabinet crisis of 1910', in A. Cosgrove and D. McCartney (eds), *Studies in Irish History* (Dublin, 1979), p. 280, 291–2.
6. Stephen Koss, *Asquith* (London, 1985 ed.), pp. 121–2.
7. Bentley, op. cit., p. 355.
8. P. Jalland, *The Liberals and Ireland* (Brighton, 1980), p. 29.
9. Richard Murphy, 'Faction in the Conservative Party and the Home Rule crisis 1912–14', *History*, Vol. 71, No. 232 (1986), pp. 222–3.
10. M. Laffan, *The Partition of Ireland, 1911–1925* (Dundalk, 1983), p. 26.
11. Bentley, op. cit., p. 365; M. Pugh, *The Tories and the People* (Oxford, 1985), p. 165.
12. M. and E. Brock, *H. H. Asquith: Letters to Venetia Stanley* (Oxford, 1982), p. 61.
13. Murphy, op. cit., p. 232.
14. Ramsden, op. cit., p. 83.
15. Koss, op. cit., p. 162.
16. D. G. Boyce, 'British Opinion, Ireland and the War, 1916–1918', in *Historical Journal*, Vol. 17, No. 3 (Sept. 1974), pp. 578–83.
17. Ibid., p. 586.
18. D. G. Boyce, 'British Conservative Opinion, The Ulster Question, and the Partition of Ireland, 1912–1921', *Irish Historical Studies*, Vol. XVII, No. 65 (March, 1970), pp. 95–6.
19. War Cabinet Minutes, 29 July 1918, Cab. 23/7.
20. Tom Jones, *Whitehall Diary* (ed. K. Middlemas), Vol. III, *Ireland, 1918–1925* (London, 1971), pp. 5–9.
21. F. S. Oliver to Lord Selborne, 23 Sept. 1918, MS. Selborne 64/140.
22. Boyce, 'British opinion, Ireland and the War', pp. 591–2.
23. Ramsden, op. cit., pp. 118–19.
24. D. G. Boyce, *Englishmen and Irish Troubles* (London, 1972), p. 47.
25. C. Townshend, *Political Violence in Ireland* (Oxford, 1983), pp. 325–326.
26. For a detailed account of the framing of the Government of Ireland Act see Richard Murphy, 'Walter Long and the making of the Government of Ireland Act, 1919–1920', *Irish Historical Studies*, Vol. XXV, No. 97 (May, 1986), pp. 82–96.
27. C. Townshend, *The British Campaign in Ireland, 1919–1921* (London, 1975), p. 191.
28. Boyce, *Englishmen and Irish Troubles*, p. 146.
29 Bryan Follis, *A State under Siege: The Establishment of Northern Ireland, 1920–1925* (Oxford, 1995), pp. 61–7.
30. Jones, op. cit., p. 166.

31 Bryan Follis, *A State under Siege*, pp. 73–7.

32. John Campbell, *F. E. Smith: 1st Earl of Birkenhead* (London, 1983), p. 579.

33. Ramsden, op. cit., p. 157.

34. Dutton, op. cit., p. 172–3.

35. T. Towey, 'The Reaction of the British Government to the 1922 Collins-de Valera pact', *Irish Historical Studies*, Vol. XXII, No. 85 (March 1980), p. 66.

36. Patrick Buckland, *The Factory of Grievances* (Dublin, 1979), pp. 198–205.

37. Patrick Buckland, *A History of Northern Ireland* (Dublin, 1981), pp. 48–9, 52–4.

38. Campbell, op. cit., p. 533.

39. John Stubbs, 'The impact of the Great War on the Conservative Party', in G. Peele and C. Cook (eds), *The Politics of Reappraisal* (London, 1975), p. 19.

CHAPTER 3

1. Martin Pugh, *The Tories and the People* (Oxford, 1985), p. 185.

2. Jones, op. cit., pp. 225–32, 236.

3. Laffan, op. cit., pp. 99–101.

4. Jones, op. cit., p. 244.

5. G. Bell, *Troublesome Business: the Labour Party and the Irish Question* (London, 1982), p. 31.

6. R. Fanning, *Independent Ireland* (Dublin, 1983), pp. 111–12.

7. W. K. Hancock, *Survey of British Commonwealth Affairs*, Vol. I, *Problems of Nationality, 1918–1936* (London, 1937), pp. 335–6.

8. Ibid., pp. 349–50.

9. *Hansard (Commons)*, Vol. 268 (4 July 1932), cols 50, 57–8.

10. Fanning, op. cit., pp. 116–17.

11. H. Montgomery Hyde, *Baldwin* (London, 1973), pp. 432–3, 523–524.

12. H. Duncan Hall, *Commonwealth* (London, 1971), pp. 816–17.

13. Deirdre McMahon, *Republicans and Imperialists; Anglo-Irish Relations in the 1930s* (Yale, 1984), p. 220.

14. R. Fisk, *In Time of War* (London, 1983), p. 33.

15. D. S. Johnson, 'Northern Ireland as a Problem in the Economic War of 1932–38', *Irish Historical Studies*, Vol. XXII, No. 86 (Sept. 1980), pp. 147–8.

16. Ibid., p. 153.

17. McMahon, op. cit., p. 241.

18. Johnson, op. cit., pp. 154–5.

19. *Patrick Buckland, The Factory of Grievances*, pp. 113–16.

20. Johnson, op. cit., pp. 159–61.

21. McMahon, op. cit., pp. 258–61.
22. Ibid., p. 282.
23. *Hansard (Commons)*, Vol. 335 (5 May 1938), cols 1071–1184.
24. John Bowman, *De Valera and the Ulster Question, 1917–1973* (Oxford, 1982), p. 182.
25. McMahon, op. cit., pp. 270–1.
26. Paul Canning, *British Policy towards Ireland, 1921–1941* (Oxford, 1985), pp. 225–7.
27. Fisk, op. cit., pp. 56–9.
28. Bowman, op. cit., pp. 189–92.
29. Canning, op. cit., pp. 243, 273.
30. Fisk, op. cit., pp. 177–85.
31. Bowman, op. cit., pp. 246–7.
32. Ibid., pp. 250–1.
33. Desmond Donnelly Papers, National Library of Wales, Box 6.
34 Brian Barton, 'Relations between Westminster and Stormont during the Attlee Premiership', in *Irish Political Studies*, Vol. 7 (1992), pp. 1–20, at pp. 2–4.
35. G. Bell, op. cit., pp. 73–7.
36. Bowman, op. cit., pp. 196–7.
37. Brian Barton, 'Relations between Westminster and Stormont during the Attlee premiership', in *Irish Political Studies*, Vol. 7 (1992), p. 12.
38. D. G. Boyce, 'From War to Neutrality: Anglo-Irish Relations, 1921–1950', *British Journal of International Studies*, 5 (1978), p. 33.
39. Brian Barton, 'Relations between Westminster and Stormont', in *Irish Political Studies*, Vol. 7 (1992), p. 19.
40. Hall, op. cit., p. 819.
41. Boyce, 'From War to Neutrality', p. 34.
42. Bell, op. cit., p. 99.

CHAPTER 4

1. D. G. Boyce, 'Ulster: Some Consequences of Devolution', *Planet*, 13 (August/September 1972), p. 6.
2. D. Harkness, *Northern Ireland since 1920* (Dublin, 1983), p. 131.
3. Paul Rose, *Backbencher's Dilemma* (London, 1981), pp. 178–9, 183.
4. Harold Wilson, *The Labour Government, 1964–1970: A Personal Record* (London, 1971), p. 270.
5. Terence O'Neill, *Autobiography* (London, 1972), p. 99.
6. Wilson, op. cit., p. 672.
7. Richard Crossman, *The Diaries of a Cabinet Minister, Vol. III: Secretary of State for Social Services, 1968–70* (London, 1977), pp. 477–8, 570, 618–9.
8. Ibid., p. 622.

9. *New Statesman*, 22 August 1969.
10. Crossman, op. cit., p. 623.
11. *Economist*, 23 August 1969.
12. Patrick Buckland, *A History of Northern Ireland* (London, 1981), p. 133.
13. B. H. Reid, 'The Experience of the British Army in Northern Ireland', in Alan O'Day and Y. Alexander, *Ireland's Terrorist Dilemma* (Dordrecht, 1986), p. 256.
14. Barry White, *John Hume: Statesman of the Troubles* (Belfast, 1984), p. 120.
15. Reid, op. cit., pp. 257–8.
16. Wilson, op. cit., p. 697.
17. Henry Patterson, 'British Governments and the "Protestant Backlash" 1969–74', in A. O'Day and Y. Alexander, *Ireland's Terrorist Dilemma*, p. 232.
18. Harold Wilson, *Final Term: the Labour Government, 1974–76* (London, 1971), p. 71.
19. Merlyn Rees, *Northern Ireland: a Personal View* (London, 1985), p. 77.
20. Reid, op. cit., pp. 258–60.
21. Wilson, *Final Term*, p. 77.
22. Ben Pimlott, *Harold Wilson* (London, 1992), p. 633.
23. Barbara Castle, *Diaries, 1974–76* (London, 1980), pp. 236–7.
24. Wilson, *Final Term*, p. 78.
25. Richard Rose, *Northern Ireland: a Time of Choice* (London, 1976), pp. 124, 126–7.
26. P. Bew and H. Patterson, *The British State and the Ulster Crisis from Wilson to Thatcher* (London, 1985), p. 87.
27. Rees, op. cit., p. 180.
28. Austen Morgan, *Harold Wilson* (London, 1992), p. 490.
29. K. Pringle, 'British Labour Party Policies in Northern Ireland', University of Bristol, B.A. Dissertation (1984), p. 60.
30. For an example see Martin Collins (ed.), *Ireland After Britain* (London, 1985), esp. p. 150.
31. Austen Morgan, *Harold Wilson*, p. 449. But by 3 June, Benn confessed that on the withdrawal question, he might 'well be in a minority' (Tony Benn, *Against The Tide: Diaries, 1973–1976* (London, 1989), p. 164.
32. *Northern Ireland: Statement of the National Executive Committee at the 1981 Conference*, pp. 7, 11.
33. Anthony Kenny, *The Road to Hillsborough* (London, 1986), p. 37.
34 Paul Bew, Peter Gibbon and Henry Patterson, *Northern Ireland, 1921–1994: Political Forces and Social Classes* (London, 1994), p. 210.
35. Ibid., Ch. 8.
36. Tom Garvin, 'The Politics of the Republic of Ireland: the Impact of the North', unpublished paper read to Conference at Keele University, March 1986, esp. p. 10.
37. Kenny, op. cit., Ch. 16.

38. Ibid., p. 103.
39. *Economist*, 'Don't Cry for Ulster', 23 November 1985.
40. Kenny, op. cit., p. 83.
41. For a survey of British public opinion in 1986 see James Naughtie, 'The View From the Other End of the Telescope', *Fortnight* (Belfast), No. 245 (November 1986), pp. 4–6, and Conor O'Cleary, 'North Slips Down Everyone's Agenda', ibid., pp. 8–10.

CHAPTER 5

1. Garret Fitzgerald, *All in a Life* (London, 1991), Ch. 16.
2. Ibid., pp. 569–70.
3. Ibid., p. 571.
4. Ibid., p. 571.
5. Ibid., p. 572.
6. Ibid., p. 573. For the British concentration on security see Margaret Thatcher, *The Downing Street Years* (London, 1993), pp. 398, 402.
7. Arwel Ellis Owen, *The Anglo-Irish Agreement: The First Three Years* (Cardiff, 1994), pp. 167, 183–5.
8. Michael Cunningham, *British Government Policy in Northern Ireland, 1969–1989: Its Nature and Execution* (Manchester, 1991), pp. 216–19.
9. Paul Bew and Gordon Gillespie, *Northern Ireland: A Chronology of the Troubles, 1968–1993* (Dublin, 1993), pp. 169–70, 206.
10. Ibid., p. 207.
11. Ibid., p. 189.
12. A. E. Owen, *The Anglo-Irish Agreement*, pp. 192–200.
13. I am indebted for this information to my postgraduate student, Mr Alan Parkinson, who is working on British perceptions of Ulster Unionism in this period.
14. Paul Dixon, ' "The Usual English Doubletalk": The British Political Parties and the Ulster Unionists, 1974–1994', in *Irish Political Studies*, Vol. 9 (1994), pp. 25–40. Michael *Cunningham, British Government Policy in Northern Ireland 1969–1989: Its Nature and Execution* pp. 198–99.
15. Ibid., p. 227.
16. Ibid., p. 240.
17. Ibid., pp. 230–31.
18. Garret Fitzgerald, *All in a Life*, p. 515.
19. Bew and Gillespie, op. cit., p. 256.
20. Ibid., pp. 276–8.
21. The speech is quoted in Seamus Deane (ed.) *The Field Day Anthology of Irish Writing* (3 Vols., Derry, 1991), Vol. 3, pp. 372–7.
22. Bew and Gillespie, *Northern Ireland: a Chronology of the Troubles*, pp. 289–90.

23. Paul Dixon, ' "The Usual English Doubletalk" ', in *Irish Political Studies*, Vol. 9 (1994), pp. 36–7.
24. Bew and Gillispie, *Northern Ireland*, pp. 297–8.
25. Private information.
26. Bew and Gillespie, *Northern Ireland*, pp. 243, 261.
27. Ibid., pp. 292–3, 296.
28. Ibid., pp. 282, 296.
29. Brian Rowan, *Behind the Lines: The Story of the IRA and Loyalist Ceasefires* (Belfast, 1995), p. 38.
30. Bew and Gillespie, *Northern Ireland*, p. 210.
31. Brian Rowan, *Behind the Lines*, p. 46.
32. M. L. R. Smith, *Fighting for Ireland? The Military Strategy of the Irish Republican Movement* (London, 1995), pp. 173–4.
33. Bew and Gillespie, *Northern Ireland*, pp. 217–18.
34. Smith, *Fighting for Ireland?* p. 198.
35. Ibid., p. 201.
36. Rowan, *Behind the Lines*, pp. 47–8.
37. Smith, op. cit., pp. 202–3.
38. Rowan, op. cit., pp. 50–53.
39. Ibid., pp. 54–5.
40. Ibid., p. 55.
41. Smith, op. cit., p. 199.
42. Ibid., pp. 205–6; Rowan, op. cit., pp. 63–71.
43. Smith, op. cit., p. 206.
44. 'Diary of events', in *Irish Political Studies*, Vol. 9 (1994), p. 244.
45. Rick Wilford and Sydney Elliott, 'The Northern Ireland Affairs Select Committee', in *Irish Political Studies*, Vol. 10 (1995), pp. 216–24.
46. Private information.
47. The full text of the Declaration is printed in D. G. Boyce, *Nationalism in Ireland*, 3rd edition (London, 1995), pp. 433–7.
48. Rowan, *Behind the Lines*, p. 83.
49. Smith, *Fighting for Ireland?*, p. 208.
50. Rowan, p. 89.
51. For the last stages of the evolution of the IRA ceasefire see Rowan, op. cit., pp. 92–101.
52. Rowan, op. cit., p. 119.
53. Ibid., p. 127.
54. *Keesings Contemporary Archives*, Vol. 40, p. 40191.
55. *The Times*, 1 February 1995.
56. Ibid.
57. Ibid., 2 February 1995. Mayhew's statement is in *Hansard* (Commons), Vol. 253 (1 February 1995), cols. 1085–1100.
58. George Drower, *John Hume: Peacemaker*, pp. 200–201.
59. *The Times*, 23 February 1995; full text on pp. 4 and 5.

60. Paul Dixon ' "The Usual English Doubletalk" ', in *Irish Political Studies*, Vol. 9 (1994), pp. 25–40.
61. James Prior, *A Balance of Power* (London, 1986), p. 193.
62. Paul Bew, Peter Gibbon and Henry Patterson, *Northern Ireland, 1921–1994: Political Forces and Social Classes* (London, 1995), p. 216. Margaret Thatcher, *The Downing Street Years*, p. 385.
63. Bew and Gillespie, *Northern Ireland*, pp. 291–2.
64. Michael Cunningham, 'Conservative Dissidents and the Irish Question: the pro-integrationist lobby, 1973–94', in *Irish Political Studies*, Vol. 10 (1995), pp. 26–42.
65. M. L. R. Smith, *Fighting for Ireland?* pp. 183–7. For useful surveys of the media and public opinion see John Kirkaldy, 'Northern Ireland and Fleet Street: Misreporting a Continuing Tragedy', and 'Terrorism, the Media and the Liberal Democratic State', in Yonah Alexander and Alan O'Day (eds), *Terrorism in Ireland* (Beckenham, Kent, 1984), Chs 9 and 11.
66. For another example, that of the Labour Government's response to the Irish state's decision to leave the Commonwealth in 1949, see Brian Barton, 'Relations between Westminster and Stormont during the Attlee Premiership', in *Irish Political Studies*, Vol. 7 (1992), pp. 1–20.
67. Drower, *John Hume*, p. 204.
68. John Campbell, *Edward Heath: A Biography* (London, 1993), p. 434.
69. For an assessment of Republicanism see Smith, *Fighting for Ireland?* pp. 219–27. The retirement of James Molyneux and his replacement by David Trimble has met with varying responses, but Trimble has already made a journey to Dublin to meet the Irish Prime Minister, John Bruton. The SDLP remains enigmatic; the Democratic Unionists, under the Reverend Ian Paisley, remain un-enigmatic, but Paisley has recently had a meeting with John Major which did not end with his ejection from the Prime Minister's office. Unionist political groups closest to the paramilitary organisations have responded to the peace moves with a studied moderation.

CONCLUSION

1. J. G. Darwin, 'Fear of Falling: British Politics and Imperial Decline since 1900', *Transaction of the Royal Historical Society*, 5th series, Vol. 36, p. 40.

EPILOGUE

1. *The Times*, 1 and 2 December 1995.

References

2. Ibid., 1 December 1995. See also the *Financial Times* Northern Ireland Survey, 30 November 1995.
3. *Belfast Telegraph*, 8 December 1995.
4. Ibid..
5. *The Times*, 2 January 1996.
6. Ibid.,
7. Ibid..

BIBLIOGRAPHICAL
AND HISTORIOGRAPHICAL
ESSAY

I

The historiography of the Irish Question and British politics has been influenced by three factors: the political relationship between Britain and Ireland; the release of new source material, and the current fashions in historical writings.

Because the Irish Question has not yet passed into history, its history is influenced by the Question. In particular, two themes emerge:

1. The notion that Irish political issues were not like any other political issues, and that when British politicians and parties came to tackle them, they were absolved of the critical appraisal normally applied to their performance in, say, trade union legislation or the budget. This created an almost non or apolitical approach to the history of the Irish Question; it was regarded as a special case, which Britain took up as an act of folly, or out of the goodness of her heart. This view owes something to Gladstone's moral sense of the Irish Question, which elevated it beyond the level of normal politics. Modern secretaries of state for Northern Ireland still shelter under its umbrella.

2. The view that the Irish Question was, and is, a dangerous and alien irruption into the British body politic, destroying the even tenor of British politics, threatening its democratic fabric, dividing its parties and even friends, and injecting the innate bitterness and violence of Irish politics into Britain. This view is encapsulated in phrases like 'That Damnable Question', the 'Irish imbroglio', or (at best) the 'Irish tragedy'.

The result was a tendency among British (or more accurately English) historians to see the Irish Question as fundamentally irrelevant to the mainstream of the British political system; and this in turn helped to create a pro-Liberal or pro-Home Rule historiography in which Unionists, Irish and British, obstinately and unreasonably 'opposed' the natural solution to the Irish Question, i.e. self-government, and a united Ireland under Dublin rule. R. C. K. Ensor's *England, 1870–1914* in the Oxford History of England series offers an elegant version of this theme; George Dangerfield's *Strange Death of Liberal England* is energetic and compelling; and these inspired a whole range of textbooks on Ireland's role in British history.

The conviction that Ireland inflicted only damage and disruption on British politics also meant that British historians tended to neglect the subject, especially in its post-1922 phase. C. L. Mowat's masterly *Britain between the Wars* (Chicago, 1955 and subsequent editions) was one of the few 'mainstream' books offering chapters on Anglo-Irish relations between 1922 and 1939. Nicholas Mansergh offered an incisive and yet sweeping interpretation in his *Ireland in the Age of Reform and Revolution* (London, 1940; republished and revised as *The Irish Question, 1840–1921*). The return of the Question in the 1960s provided much employment for political scientists, but did not encourage a new Mansergh: there was no major historical treatment of the whole episode, nor of its more recent manifestations in British politics. Partly this is because of the paucity of sources, for official records and private papers are still of course undisclosed, and the publication of some diaries, like that of Richard Crossman (1977) reveal the flavour of the British reaction, but not enough of its substantive detail.

But this is certainly not true of the earlier period between 1868 and 1923, and, more recently, up to 1950. For the release of major British archives, especially the official cabinet papers, the Lloyd George and Bonar Law papers, and a host of other collections has enabled historians to investigate thoroughly the formulation of Irish policy in these crucial years. The result has been a flood of monographs and articles which constitute a major piece of revisionism in British and Irish history, e.g. over the partition of Ireland. These sources have been reinforced by the publication of important political diaries such as Tom Jones' *Whitehall Diary* (Vol. III, Oxford, 1971) and letters such as Asquith's correspondence with Venetia Stanley (eds M. and E. Brock, Oxford, 1982). The Gladstone era still awaits the publication of the later diaries, but the volumes so far released are a valuable insight into the thinking of the first major British statesman to take Ireland seriously since Sir Robert Peel.

Because Ireland was regarded as atypical of British political life, it was some time before historical fashion was applied to Ireland by 'mainstream' British historians. When it was, however, it was applied with a vengeance. First of all Gladstone's high moral purpose was transformed by John Vincent into low political cunning. Then Lloyd George's Irish policy was placed under the microscope of the 'High Politics' school and it was claimed that Lloyd George and his contemporaries saw Ireland as part of the great political game, an issue to be raised or set aside according to the needs of ambitious politicians. This was a healthy corrective to the older view that

British politicians (or at any rate Liberal politicians) were unaffected by such vulgar considerations when it came to Ireland. But the view was pressed too far; and a more realistic, more fully rounded assessment of the interplay of parties, voters and leaders is needed (and in some cases has been attempted) to enable a convincing picture of the complexities of the Irish Question and British politics to be written.

II

The role of Gladstone in Irish affairs still awaits the full assessment which the publication of all the diaries, and of the second volume of Richard Shannon's biography will render possible (his first volume stops in 1865). But there are many articles and essays which help reconstruct the labyrinthine Gladstonian path towards Irish disestablishment, land reform and Home Rule. Of special interest is the work of E. D. Steele: 'Gladstone and Ireland,' *Irish Historical Studies*, XVII (1970); 'Gladstone, Irish Violence, and Conciliation', in A. Cosgrove (ed.), *Studies in Irish History* (Dublin, 1979); and his book *Irish Land and British Politics: Tenant Right and Nationality, 1865–1870* (Cambridge, 1974). John Vincent's *Gladstone and Ireland* (Raleigh lecture, London, 1977) corrects, and is corrected by J. L. Hammond's *Gladstone and the Irish Nation* (London, 1964 ed.), Alan O'Day, *Parnell and the First Home Rule Episode* (Dublin, 1986), is a detailed and balanced study; J. Loughlin, *Gladstone, Home Rule, and the Ulster Question* (Dublin, 1986) sometimes pushes the argument too far, but generally steers a neat course between 'high' and 'low' politics.

The Conservative and Unionist response deserves a fuller treatment than it has received. The latest work is A. Gailey, *Ireland and the Death of Kindness: the Experience of Constructive Unionism, 1890–1905* (Cork, 1987), but L. P. Curtis' *Coercion and Conciliation in Ireland, 1880–1892* (Princeton, 1963) is a necessary complement. Patrick Buckland's *Irish Unionism I: the Anglo-Irish and the New Ireland, 1885–1922* (Dublin, 1972) demonstrated the importance of Irish Unionists to British politics in general and the Conservative Party in particular. Peter Davis, 'The Liberal Unionist Party and the Irish Policy of Lord Salisbury's Government, 1886–92', *Historical Journal*, XVIII (1975) is a useful specialist study. The attempt by Liberals and Unionists alike to formulate new Irish policies between 1903 and 1908 is traced by Alan O'Day, 'Irish Home Rule and Liberalism', in *The Edwardian Age: Conflict and Stability* (London, 1979). The Home Rule crisis of 1912–14 has been treated in considerable detail, using a wide variety of sources: Pat Jalland's *The Liberals and Ireland: the Ulster Question in British Politics to 1914* (Brighton, 1980); I. F. W. Beckett's *The Army and the Curragh Incident, 1914* (London, 1986), and an article by Richard Murphy, 'Faction in the Conservative

179

Party and the Home Rule Crisis, 1912–14', *History*, Vol. 71 (1986), offer the latest research. The impact of the Irish Question in the Great War is examined in J. M. McEwan 'The Liberal Party and the Irish Question', *Journal of British Studies*, XII (1972) and A. J. Ward, 'Lloyd George and the 1918 Conscription Crisis', *Historical Journal*, XVII (1974) and more generally by D. G. Boyce 'British opinion, Ireland and the War', *Historical Journal*, XVII (1974). S. Lawlor, *Britain and Ireland, 1914–1923* (Dublin, 1983), is important for its detailed description of official thinking on the Irish Question. Richard Murphy, 'Walter Long and the Government of Ireland Act', *Irish Historical Studies*, XXV (1986), and D. G. Boyce, *Englishmen and Irish Troubles* (London, 1972), examine the dilemmas facing the British government, while Charles Townshend, *The British Campaign in Ireland* (Oxford, 1975) studies the civil-military angle.

P. Canning, *British Policy Towards Ireland, 1921–1941* (Oxford, 1985) is based on a wide range of private papers; see also D. Harkness, 'England's Irish Question', in C. Cook and G. Peele (eds), *The Politics of Reappraisal* (London, 1975). An older work is still indispensable: W. K. Hancock's *Survey of British Commonwealth Affairs*, Vol. I, *Problems of Nationality, 1918–1936* (London, 1937) is extraordinarily fresh, but must be read with D. McMahon's *Republicans and Imperialists: Anglo-Irish Relations in the 1930s* (Yale, 1984). John Ramsden, *The Age of Balfour and Baldwin* (London, 1978), is full of insightful comments on the Conservative Party's Unionist phase. Robert Fisk, *In Time of War* (London, 1983) offers a full treatment of the effect of the Second World War on British attitudes to Ireland; G. Bell looks with a jaundiced eye on Attlee's Irish policy and indeed on Labour policy generally in his *Troublesome Business* (London, 1982), but uses important documents to do so.

The return of the Question in the 1960s has produced a massive literature on Northern Ireland, much of it ephemeral. Exceptions are P. Bew and H. Patterson, *The British State and the Ulster Crisis: from Wilson to Thatcher* (London, 1985) which is well researched and forcefully written, but suffers from a failure to define or consider what the British 'state' is. J. Bulpitt's *Territory and Power in the United Kingdom* (Manchester, 1983) places the Irish Question in its British context and offers interesting comparisons with the rest of the 'Celtic' fringe. Two other works of a Pan-Celtic kind are V. Bogdanor, *Devolution* (Oxford, 1979) and A. H. Birch, *Political Integration and Disintegration in the British Isles* (London, 1977). Richard Rose's work is always valuable; see his 'The United Kingdom as a multi-national state' (Glasgow, 1970) which raised a few eyebrows, and should be compulsory reading for the inhabitants of Hampstead (and not only Hampstead). Anthony Kenny, *The Road to Hillsborough* (London, 1986) is a clear account of the prologue to the latest effort at an Anglo-Irish political process.

Finally biographies, diaries and the like offer chapters or sections on the

Irish Question and British politics. Most useful are S. Koss, *Asquith* (London, 1985 ed.); John Campbell, *F. E. Smith, First Earl of Birkenhead* (London, 1983); Lord Blake, *The Unknown Prime Minister: the Life and Times of Andrew Bonar Law* (London, 1955); John Grigg, *Lloyd George: the People's Champion* (London, 1978) and *From Peace to War* (London, 1985); D. Dutton, *Austen Chamberlain: Gentleman in Politics* (Bolton, 1985); Martin Gilbert, *W. S. Churchill* (Vols IV–VI, London, 1975–83); H. Montgomery Hyde, *Baldwin* (London, 1973); Harold Wilson, *The Labour Government: a personal record, 1964–70* (London, 1971); James Callaghan, *A House Divided* (London, 1973); Richard Crossman, *Diaries of a Cabinet Minister* (Vol. III, London, 1977). Conservatives have, however, been less forthcoming with personal reminiscences, James Prior's *A Balance of Power* (London, 1986) being something of an exception. The Tory habit of discretion gives the historian of the Irish Question and British politics food for thought, but not for research and analysis. But Padraig O'Malley's, *The Uncivil Wars: Ireland Today* (Belfast, 1983) lets the politicians (including British politicians) speak for themselves with much profit, but little comfort, for the reader.

UPDATE

The last decade has seen the publication of important work on the historical and contemporary dimensions of this subject. A major landmark is the completion of Colin Matthew's formidable edition of the Gladstone diaries, with accompanying official and private papers. Volumes X, 1881–1883 (Oxford, 1990); XI, 1883–1886 (Oxford, 1990); XII, 1887–1891 (Oxford, 1994); and XIII, 1892–1896 (Oxford, 1994) are indispensable for an understanding of Gladstone's Home Rule and land policies – even if they confirm J. L. Hammond's views, first put forward decades ago: that Gladstone meant business on the Irish question. T. A. Jenkins, *Gladstone, Whiggery and the Liberal Party, 1874–1886* (Oxford, 1988) is something of a constraint on this view, but is perfectly compatible with it. Alvin Jackson, *The Ulster Party: Irish Unionists in the House of Commons, 1884–1911* (Oxford, 1989) has important material on the relationship between the Unionists and the Conservative party. David Dutton, *His Majesty's Loyal Opposition: The Unionist Party in Opposition, 1905–1915* (Liverpool, 1992) has much on Ireland; and Nicholas Mansergh, *The Unresolved Question: The Anglo-Irish Settlement and its undoing* (New Haven and London, 1991) is Mansergh's last words on a subject to which he has always brought much enlightenment. There is plenty of Irish material in D. G. Boyce (ed.), *The Crisis of British Unionism: The Domestic Political papers of the Second Earl of Selborne, 1885–1922* (London, 1987); and in another publication of The Historians' Press: Philip Williamson (ed.), *The Modernisation of Conservative Politics: The Diaries and*

Letters of William Bridgeman, 1904–1935 (London, 1988). John Kendle, *Ireland and the Federal Solution: the Debate over the United Kingdom Constitution, 1870–1921* (Kingston and Montreal, 1989), and his *Walter Long* (Dublin, 1992) show how the Irish Question meshed with the wider British question of parliamentary government; his study of Long is an example of how a staunch Unionist could change his mind on Ireland as the context changed. Catherine B. Shannon, *Arthur J. Balfour and Ireland, 1874–1922* traces the political views of a key Conservative and Unionist figure. Peter Collins (ed.), *Nationalism and Unionism: Conflict in Ireland, 1885–1921* (Belfast: Institute of Irish Studies, 1994) contains good essays. Bryan Follis, *A State under Siege: the Establishment of Northern Ireland, 1920–1925* (Oxford, 1995) shows the British Government's tentative relationship with the state. An important and thoroughly researched essay is Brian Barton's 'Relations between Westminster and Stormont during the Attlee Premiership' in *Irish Political Studies*, Vol. 7 (1992), pp. 1–20.

In the contemporary field, Michael Cunningham's *British Government Policy in Northern Ireland, 1969–1989* (Manchester, 1991) is a sober and critical analysis. Brian Rowan, *Behind the Lines: The Story of the I. R. A. and Loyalist Ceasefires* (Belfast, 1995) is detailed and convincing. M. L. R. Smith, *Fighting for Ireland? The Military Strategy of the Irish Republican Movement* (London, 1995), although its focus is on the Irish side, is essential for an understanding of what the British government has been trying to grapple with, both militarily and politically. Brigid Hadfield, 'Northern Ireland affairs at Westminster', in P. Roche and B. Barton (eds), *The Northern Ireland Question: Myths and Reality* (Aldershot, 1991) is a close analysis of a subject that is more complex than it first appears. Paul Bew, Peter Gibbon and Henry Patterson, *The State in Northern Ireland, 1921–1994* (London, 1994) is a revised version of an earlier book, and contains much new material.

Politicians' autobiographies roll out, and most of them contain useful information for those willing to wade through their self-justificatory pages. Garret Fitzgerald's, *All in a Life: an Autobiography* (London, 1991), though of course centred on Irish politics, contains much information about British policy, and especially the making of the Anglo-Irish Agreement. Margaret Thatcher, *The Downing Street Years* (London, 1993) is less full, but still of great interest; D. G. Boyce attempts a summary of her views in his 'The Irish Connection', in Dennis Kavanagh and Anthony Seldon (eds), *The Thatcher Effect* (Oxford, 1989), pp. 226–38. William Whitelaw, *The Whitelaw Memoirs* (London, 1989) covers his significant role in an especially turbulent period. James Prior, *A Balance of Power* (London, 1986) has a section on his term of office as Northern Ireland Secretary, in which he expresses his low opinion of Ulster Unionist political leaders even in a time when they were supposed to have made their way back into the Conservative good books. On the Labour side Tony Benn, *Against the Tide: Diaries, 1973–1976* (London, 1989) describes the foundering Wilson Cabinet at a key moment in Northern Ireland's political history. Biographies of Wilson by Ben Pimlott (London, 1992) and Austen Morgan (London, 1992) throw light on this era, especially Morgan's, which is more detailed on Ulster policy and has the insider's eye for what is significant. John Campbell, *Edward Heath* (London, 1993) is good on the making of the Sunningdale Agreement.

The launching of the journal *Irish Political Studies* some years ago has resulted in a series of high-quality articles on the contemporary scene. Among the best are Feargal Cochrane, 'Progressive or Regressive? The Anglo-Irish Agreement as a dynamic in the Northern Ireland Polity', Vol. 8 (1993), pp. 1–20; Paul Dixon, ' "The Usual English Doubletalk": The British political parties and the Ulster Unionists. 1974–1994', Vol. 9 (1994), pp. 25–40; Michael Cunningham, 'Conservative Dissidents and the Irish Question: the pro-integrationist lobby, 1973–1994', Vol. 10 (1995). See also Feargal Cochrane, 'Any Takers? The Isolation of Northern Ireland', in *Political Studies*, Vol. 42 (1994), pp. 378–98; W. Harvey Cox, 'Public Opinion and the Anglo-Irish Agreement', in *Government and Opposition*, Vol. 22 (1987), pp. 336–51; Paul Arthur, 'The Anglo-Irish Joint Declaration: Towards a Lasting Peace?', Ibid., Vol. 29 (1994), pp. 218–30.

Finally, mention must be made of Paul Bew and Gordon Gillespie, *Northern Ireland: A Chronology of The Troubles, 1969–1993* (Dublin, 1993). This is much more than a mere list of dates. It is studded with important quotations, together with an exhaustive diary of events, and a series of short, incisive essays on particular issues. It forms the basis of any writing on the Northern Ireland question over the past 25 years, and contains much material on British political attitudes and decisions. It is indispensable.

APPENDIX A

IMPORTANT BRITISH AND IRISH GENERAL ELECTION RESULTS, 1868–1918

1868:	Great Britain:	Liberals	321
		Conservatives	232
	Ireland:	Liberals	66
		Conservatives	39

1874:	Great Britain:	Liberals	232
		Conservatives	317
	Ireland:	Home Rulers	60
		Liberals	10
		Conservatives	33

1885:	Great Britain:	Liberals	335
		Conservatives	231
		Irish Nationalist	1
		(Scotland Div., Liverpool)	
	Ireland:	Home Rulers	85
		Conservatives	18

(Nationalist strength equal to Liberals majority over the Conservatives; Parnell can keep either British party out of office, but can only put the Liberals in.)

1886:	Great Britain:	Liberals	191
		Unionists	300
		Liberal Unionists	75
		Irish Nationalist	1
	Ireland:	Home Rulers	84
		Liberal Unionists	2
		Unionists	17
1910	Great Britain:	Liberals	274
(Jan.–Feb.):		Unionists	223
		Liberal Unionists	29

184

		Irish Nationalist	1
		Labour	40
	Ireland:	Home Rulers	70
		Independent Nationalists	11
		Liberals	1
		Unionists	21
1910 (Dec.):	Great Britain:	Liberals	270
		Unionists	221
		Liberal Unionists	33
		Irish Nationalist	1
		Labour	42
	Ireland:	Home Rulers	73
		Independent Nationalists	10
		Liberals	1
		Unionists	19
1918:	Great Britain:	Coalition Liberals	133
		Coalition Unionists	335
		Coalition Labour	10
		Conservatives	23
		Liberals	28
		Labour	63
	Ireland:	Sinn Fein	73
		Home Rulers	7
		Unionists	25

(Source: *A New History of Ireland*, Vol. VIII, *A Chronology of Irish History to 1976*, Oxford, 1982.)

MAJOR ANGLO-IRISH REFORM MEASURES, CONSTITUTIONAL PROPOSALS AND AGREEMENTS, 1868–1995

1869, Irish Church Act: Disestablished and partly disendowed the Protestant episcopal Church (effective 1 Jan 1871). Provided for a representative body (synod) for the government of the Church and a body (representative church body) to administer the finances of the Church. Also provided for the purchase of church lands by tenants.

1870–81, Irish land legislation: Landlord and Tenants (Ireland) Act 1870, sought to give tenants the right to compensation for eviction and for improvements made with the landlord's consent. Treasury loans were advanced to encourage the purchase of holdings. Land Law (Ireland) Act, 1881, legalised the 'Three F's' (fair rent, free sale and fixity of tenure) throughout Ireland and established a commission to assess fair rents.

1886, First Home Rule Bill: Proposed an Irish parliament consisting of two houses, with an executive responsible to it. Empowered to make laws for the 'peace, order and good government of Ireland', but was not to legislate on the Crown, war and peace, armed forces, foreign relations, treason, trade, postage, coinage. RIC to be under control of Lord Lieutenant for two years and thereafter until arrangements made by Irish parliament. Irish MPs were to be removed entirely from the Westminster parliament.

1885–1903, Irish land legislation: Ashbourne's Act (1885) provided loans for tenants to cover the whole purchase price of land, at 4 per cent over 49 years, 1891 Balfour's Act provided much larger capital for purchase. Wyndham's Act (1903) provided bonuses to encourage landlords to sell if three-quarters of tenants agreed. Total of £83 million eventually advanced at 3 1/4 per cent over 68 1/2 years. Land acts under the Union led to the purchase of over 11 million acres at a cost of £100 million.

1893, Second Home Rule Bill: Chief difference from the 1886 Bill was that now 80 Irish MPs were to remain at Westminster, but they were forbidden to vote on purely 'British' issues.

1914, Home Rule Act: Provided for bicameral legislature, but with wide powers over revenue and defence reserved to Westminster. Irish represented at Westminster by 42 MPs. The act was passed with the proviso that it was not to be implemented until after the war, and must include amending legislation to deal with the Ulster Question.

1920, Government of Ireland Act: Partitioned Ireland into two states, each with its own Home Rule parliament, one for the six counties of Northern Ireland (Antrim, Armagh, Down, Fermanagh, Londonderry and Tyrone) and one for southern Ireland. Each parliament had strictly limited powers, and was to be elected by proportional representation. Westminster retained ultimate sovereignty and power over 'excepted' matters, such as the Crown, armed forces, coinage and external trade. A 'Council of Ireland' was provided consisting of representatives from each parliament to act as a unifying bridge.

1921, Anglo-Irish Treaty: The Irish Free State became a dominion with the same constitutional status in the British Empire as Canada, Australia, New Zealand and South Africa. Irish MPs were to take an oath of allegiance to the Crown. A governor general was appointed. The treaty formally included Northern Ireland but gave her the power of opting out of the Free State, which she promptly exercised. A 'Boundary Commission' would then be established to delineate the final border of Northern Ireland.

1925, Boundary Commission: Provided for a redrawing of the Northern Ireland state boundary in accordance with the wishes of the inhabitants, but also in the light of economic and geographical conditions. The Commission was boycotted by the Northern Ireland government, and in the end proposed only minor adjustments to the border. It was never implemented, and instead the Free State accepted a cash settlement in lieu of a boundary change.

1938, Anglo-Irish Agreements: Made between Neville Chamberlain and the government of Eamon de Valera, concerning trade, finance and the 'treaty ports' whose use Britain had retained under the 1921 Treaty. Britain's decision to cede the ports ensured Eire's neutrality in the Second World War. Northern Ireland was not a party to the agreements, but was promised the compensation of a greater share in British defence contracts, because the trade arrangements were damaging to her economy.

1949, Ireland Act: Passed by the Labour government in response to Eire's decision to leave the Commonwealth. Declared that the new Republic of Ireland was not part of HM's dominions but that it was not to be regarded as a foreign country, nor its citizens to be regarded as aliens in the United

Kingdom or the colonies. Also that in no circumstances would Northern Ireland or any part thereof cease to be a part of HM's dominions without the consent of the Northern Ireland parliament.

1969, Downing Street Declaration: A joint communiqué issued by Northern Ireland and British ministers in London. Declared that the general officer commanding Northern Ireland would have overall responsibility for security. Affirmed that: (1) Northern Ireland would not cease to be part of the United Kingdom without the consent of its people and parliament; (2) Northern Ireland affairs were a matter of domestic jurisdiction; (3) the U.K. government had the ultimate responsibility for the protection of the people of Northern Ireland; (4) troops had been temporarily provided to discharge that responsibility; (5) the U.K. government welcomed the reforms introduced by the Northern Ireland government and both governments considered it vital to maintain the momentum of reform; (6) both governments were committed to the same equality of treatment for all citizens in Northern Ireland as obtained in the rest of the U.K.; (7) both governments were determined to restore normality in Northern Ireland.

1973, Northern Ireland Assembly Act: Followed the British decision to suspend the government of Northern Ireland in 1972. Provided for a single chamber assembly of 78 members to be elected by the single transferable vote.

1973, Northern Ireland Constitution Act: Reaffirmed the guarantee to the Ulster Unionists of 1949, but declared that there was to be an executive responsible to the Northern Ireland Assembly which was 'widely acceptable throughout the community'. The Assembly and Executive were to have no power over 'excepted matters' – Crown, international relations, armed forces, nationality, special powers against terrorism, the police, the appointment and dismissal of judges. Other powers were transferable to the Executive at the discretion of the secretary of state for Northern Ireland. A power-sharing executive was appointed in November 1973, a coalition of those Unionists led by Brian Faulkner, the mainly Catholic Social Democratic and Labour Party, and the Alliance Party. Brian Faulkner was appointed chief executive and Gerry Fitt as his deputy.

1973 (December), Sunningdale Conference: Held between British and Irish governments and leaders of the Northern Ireland parties in the new Executive. Agreed that there was an 'Irish Dimension' to the Ulster Problem, and set up a 'Council of Ireland' with 7 ministers from each side forming a council of ministers and a 60-member Consultative Assembly, elected half by the Dail and half by the Assembly. The Irish government agreed that 'there could be no change in the status of Northern Ireland until a majority of the people of Northern Ireland desired a change in that status'. Approved by the Northern Ireland Assembly by 43 votes to 27.

Direct rule by Britain ended on 1 Jan 1974, but the Northern Ireland executive fell after four months following a fourteen-day general strike and direct rule was resumed.

1985, Anglo-Irish Agreement: Reached after consultations between the British and Irish governments. Took the SDLP's views into consideration but excluded the Ulster Unionists. Followed the third of a series of meetings of heads of government in the Anglo-Irish Intergovernmental Council. Provided for a new intergovernmental conference which would be concerned with Northern Ireland and the relations between the two parts of the island of Ireland. Affirmed that any change in the status of Northern Ireland must be with the consent of the majority, but failed to define what the present status of Northern Ireland was – on which Great Britain and Ireland had different views, since under articles 2 and 3 of the Irish Constitution Northern Ireland was regarded as part of the Irish state. The new conference would discuss security and related matters, legal matters, including the administration of justice, and the promotion of cross-border cooperation. The agreement also supported the return of a devolved government to Northern Ireland.

1993 (December), Downing Street Declaration: This was produced against a background of a proposal drawn up between John Hume, leader of the SDLP and Gerry Adams, the Sinn Fein president; an alarming escalation of violence; and pressure upon the Dublin and London governments to intervene in what seemed to many to be a dangerous political vacuum in Northern Ireland policy. John Major and Albert Reynolds made an agreed statement which was intended to bring an end to violence. The Declaration contained concessions from both sides. The British reaffirmed that they had no selfish, strategic or economic interest in Northern Ireland but declared that it would uphold the democratic wish of a greater number of the people in Northern Ireland on the issue of whether they prefer to support the Union or a sovereign united Ireland. The Irish declared that it would be wrong to attempt to impose a united Ireland in the absence of the freely given consent of a majority of its people. Civil rights were to be secured. The Irish Taoiseach committed himself to examining any elements in Irish life which were inconsistent with a pluralist society. Both governments pledged themselves to supporting Irish unification if in the future a majority of the people were persuaded to desire this. In the event of an overall settlement, the Taoiseach was to put forward and support changes in the Irish constitution which would fully reflect the principle of consent in Northern Ireland. Both governments committed themselves to working for institutions and structures which, while respecting diversity, would enable the people of Ireland to work together in their common interest. Violence must end permanently. The Irish government would establish a 'Forum for Peace and Reconciliation' to help create trust between the Unionist and nationalist traditions. The Declaration ended with an appeal to all sides in the conflict to break the cycle of violence and the suffering it entailed.

1995 (February), The 'Framework' Document: This was drafted after the IRA and Loyalist ceasefires of August and October 1994. It was announced at Hillsborough, Co. Down, on 22 February by John Major and the new Irish Taoiseach, John Bruton. It proposed a new Northern Ireland Assembly elected by Proportional Representation with wide-ranging legislative powers. There would be a North–South body of elected representatives of the Northern Ireland Assembly and the Irish Parliament. The Republic agreed to take steps to end the Irish Constitution's Articles laying claim to sovereignty over Northern Ireland. There would be a parliamentary forum of representatives from North and South to hold wider discussions. There would be changes in British law to recognise the right of the people of Northern Ireland to decide their future, whether they would opt for the Union or a united Ireland. Referenda in both North and South would be held with a majority needed in both parts of Ireland to approve the implementation of proposals for a settlement. Both Governments committed themselves to guaranteeing civil, social and cultural rights in Northern Ireland. There would be increased cooperation between London and Dublin through the standing Inter-Governmental Conference, but this would have no right to interfere with the Northern Ireland Assembly. There would be 'harmonisation' of certain activities and services such as agriculture, industrial development, consumer affairs, transport, energy and education. John Major reaffirmed that 'nothing in these frameworks will be imposed' and that he was 'not a persuader for a united Ireland'. John Bruton declared that 'what this document is designed to do is to create new structures to which both communities in Northern Ireland will be able to give an equal sense of allegiance'.

INDEX